Mars

1	2	3	4	5	6	7
8	9	10	11	12	13	14
15	16	17	18	19	20	21
22	23	24	25	26	27	28
29	30	31				

Avril

1	2	3	4	5	6	7
8	9	10	11	12	13	14
15	16	17	18	19	20	21
22	23	24	25	26	27	28
29	30					

Juillet

1	2	3	4	5	6	7
8	9	10	11	12	13	14
15	16	17	18	19	20	21
22	23	24	25	26	27	28
29	30	31				

Aout

1	2	3	4	5	6	7
8	9	10	11	12	13	14
15	16	17	18	19	20	21
22	23	24	25	26	27	28
29	30	31				

Novembre

1	2	3	4	5	6	7
8	9	10	11	12	13	14
15	16	17	18	19	20	21
22	23	24	25	26	27	28
29	30					

Decembre

1	2	3	4	5	6	7
8	9	10	11	12	13	14
15	16	17	18	19	20	21
22	23	24	25	26	27	28
29	30	31				

THE NOSTRADAMUS
ASTROLOGICAL
DATE BOOK
1990

THE NOSTRADAMUS

ASTROLOGICAL DATE BOOK 1990

BLOOMSBURY

First published in Great Britain in 1989
by Bloomsbury Publishing Ltd.,
2 Soho Square, London W1V 5DE

ISBN 07475 0425 3

The Nostradamus Astrological Date Book 1990
was produced by Labyrinth Publishing S.A. Switzerland
Designed by Cinzia Chiari
Photographic Editors: Manuela Dunn-Mascetti & Stephane Picard
Copyright © Text 1989 by Labyrinth Publishing S.A.
All rights reserved
Printed in Hong Kong by C & C Offset Printing Co., Ltd.
Color separation by Studio Leonardo Fotolito, Florence, Italy
Typesetting by Linograf, Florence, Italy
First edition

CONTENTS

THE PROPHET

NOSTRADAMUS' DATE BOOK was probably the longest single "document" in the history of mankind, for it spanned thousands of years and almost all of it stretched into a time far beyond his own.

For those who have enjoyed *Nostradamus and the Millennium*, it must be clear exactly what an extraordinary genius this unique prophet was and how his predictions have influenced lives from the 16th century till today. And that is only the beginning, for Nostradamus' predictions run forward from our own time way into the next several millennia.

Each year, then, during the rest of this millennium, the Nostradamus Date Book will reflect the prophet's words and give some flavor of his life, combining astrological information which was created by him and also much charting of the stars which gives the reader and user of the Date Book a chance to create a time-line of his or her own personal life.

Personal horoscope information is given at the beginning of each month so that before entering events or appointments, the diary keeper may look and see how the future is likely to unfold.

We might imagine Michel de Nostredame seated at his table in the small house in Salon, France, writing the journals of the future in much the same way as we do – except that the scale is somewhat different! Whereas we might be concerned about attempting, often unsuccessfully, to map our coming week, Nostradamus was able, through his charting of the stars, to map a whole life time.

As the "Celestial Scientist" of the 16th century, he was consulted by royalty and priest, layman and professional alike, to give the benefit of his extraordinary sight. And at this time in our history, the future was equally important as a device for securing fears as it is today.

For during the early 1500s one of the world's worst plagues hit Europe with such a force that most leaders believed the world would soon end. Today we face the same dire and frightening prospect, with the ever-present dangers of nuclear war, the disasters of pollution and natural chaos and a life-style which has many areas of uncertainty, so that any form of future prediction gives us an opportunity to settle our lives within a world that is not constructed securely.

In this, the first Date Book, we will look a little at Nostradamus' life but largely in relation to the way he viewed the future – his religious environment, for example, would have strongly flavored the way in which he saw the future developing.

But mainly we will be concerned, in the text of this book, to examine how some of the predictions worked out, why some of them were more successful than others and where we may have generally made mistakes in our interpretation of the master's words.

Much of what Nostradamus tells us about our own times and our future is shadowed in language that is hard to be certain of. He wrote his "quatrains" in several languages; Provence, Latin, Greek and Italian, very often mixing them together in one piece of text. He also used anagrams, riddles and verses to further confuse the reader, making matters still worse with a crabbed and complex handwriting style which could often not be read at all!

Nevertheless, within this extraordinary complexity of expression, so many of his predictions have proven accurate that any one studying the works of the

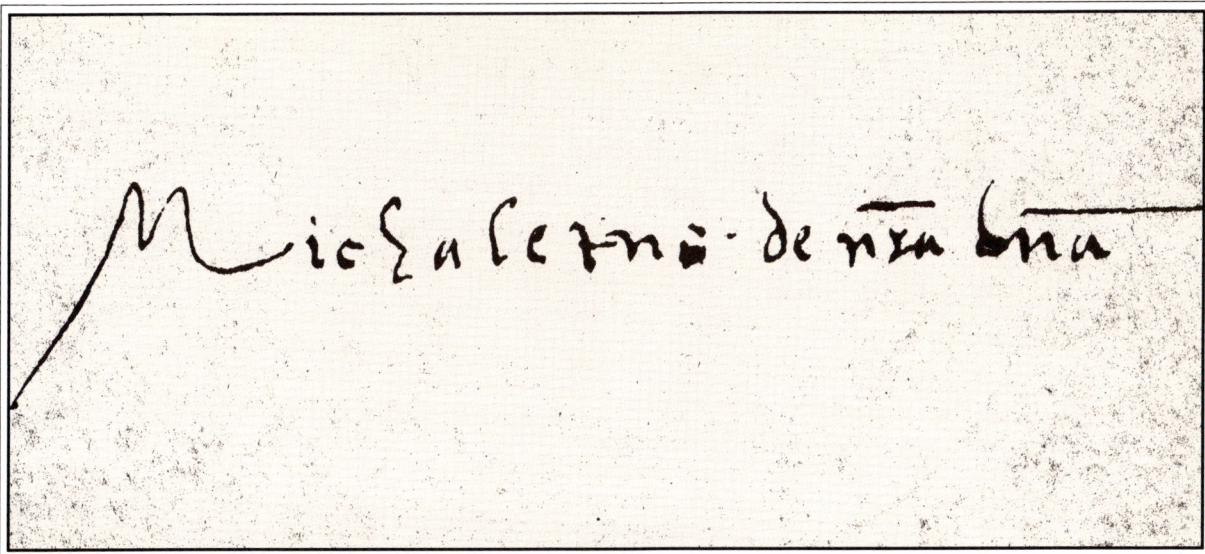

prophet must remain quite stunned by his abilities and since the 16th century there has not been anyone to equal him.

In the original book *Nostradamus and the Millennium* we concentrated largely on the predictions applying to the end of the 20th century, as this is a time rich with possibilities – a time which Nostradamus concentrated on, almost as much as he did on his own time. But he was also fascinated by the next centuries after the end of the 20th century, so that much material exists relating to our less immediate future.

Within this first Date Book then, we will look extensively at the 21st century – the time to come after we pass over the year 2,000 – to see what might stand ahead of us then.

We can presume that Nostradamus' predictions will be none the less accurate than they have been with this century. During the compilation of *Millennium* the author and the editors were personally involved in the shock of discovering this accuracy, for while in the midst of working on the chapters concerned with the years between 1986 and 1988, the prophet's words surrounding Khaddafi and the attack on the US fleet in the Gulf of Sidra actually unfolded before our eyes! Further predictions were made that applied to the same areas of attack – between the Moslem world and the United States and Europe – "The melting of a great fleet... Because of a heat as great as the Sun's the fish will be almost cooked."

According to Nostradamus, the attacks in the Mediterranean Sea were only the beginning of a war that would gradually escalate until the early 1990s when a much larger threat would be seen.

In addition, we will look at the world's religions, a subject close to all our hearts, and one that occupied much interest in *Millennium*, for some changes have occurred since first publication of the book which can be examined now in this Date Book.

So, beside being a book to record our own observations and plans for the future, *The Nostradamus Astrological Date Book* can be a simple guide to the words of one of the world's most eccentric and extraordinary Prophets, and hopefully we may be able, as the years pass by, to watch the future unfold in front of us!

THE ASTROLOGER

NOSTRADAMUS was many things; a magician, a futurologist, a doctor and even a maker of great jams! But first and foremost he was an astrologer – a scientist of the influence of the planets and stars in our skies – and it was this science, one of the most revered of his time, that led him to make the extraordinary predictions which still touch us today.

The methods used by Nostradamus are still in use amongst modern astrologers and in order to give some brief idea of how he worked, the following is an explanation of astrological systems. These systems were then applied by the Master astrologer to bring indications of future trends.

The majority of us are most impressed by astrology's ability to predict the future, for this is clearly its drama. But prediction comes from a deep, understanding of the science of astrology.

For, at its source, this science can lead us deep into our souls, it can help us understand ourselves, and it is this understanding that forms the very core of the professional astrologer's ability. For you cannot expect to predict future events if you do not know how people change and react to life.

The first step in any astrological reading is to calculate a chart giving the position of the planets and the Houses in each Zodiacal sign at the time of birth – this is called the "natal chart." The planet positions and the combinations between them will influence us in the way we act and feel and the way we are affected by the outside world. These combinations give us abilities, talents, opportunities or lessons in learning, depending on their position.

The natal chart is divided into twelve sections or "Houses." Each of these Houses denotes an area of influence.

All through our lives as the planets continue their course, they are coloring our natal chart and influencing our lives, making us take decisions, changing our inner urges and feelings, and creating situations that will be lessons along the path.

When we understand this process, it is easier to accept ourselves and enjoy our lives more fully.

But the horoscope is never a fixed thing that we remain stuck with.

In the first place we must depend a lot upon the interpretation of the astrologer, for each expert will have his own variation on the chart even though the basic information remains the same. Secondly, and most of all, the changes depend on each of us as individuals; on what we make of our lives and how we grow through our conscious awareness of life. Nothing is beyond possibility, once we see and understand an adverse aspect of life we are 99% on the way to freeing ourselves from it or understanding its implications.

The positions of the planets given in the agenda are based on Universal Time (UT), the same as Greenwich Mean time (GMT). They are given at hour zero of each Sunday, throughout 1990. To find out the influences at any given time, compare the transiting planets on the day in question with their positions and the House they go through at the time of your birth (see *Planets in Transit* by Robert Hand, Para Research or *The Changing Sky: The Dynamic New Astrology for Everyone* by Steven Forrest, Bantam). Compare the transits with the influences you feel upon yourself at that moment and soon you will be able to get a sense of how each planet combination works. Once you get the knack of it, you can then be warned of coming moods and changes in your life.

The transit of slower moving planets, such as Saturn, Uranus, Neptune and Pluto, will be felt over a longer period of time and on the contrary the faster moving planets, such as Venus and Mercury, will only be felt for a short time. Usually for a major change to occur a combination of two or more similar influences are needed.

When you see a Horoscope in a magazine or a newspaper, it has been calculated by making a chart of the transiting planets, i.e. those planets that are moving through the sky on that day, week or month, depending on the scope of the reading. These transiting planets are then compared with the Sun-sign at birth, this is the sign which we identify as "I am a Scorpio or a Sagittarius." Therefore only a partial and inaccurate judgment can be made from this method.

Comparing the transiting planets with the whole chart, a more precise and detailed interpretation can be made. In this way you can study your own life, as well as events touching a whole country or the whole Earth, as Nostradamus did 450 years ago.

THE PLANETS

THE SUN represents our desires. The position of the Sun in the chart, gives us our personality, our self, our ego. It governs the masculine, out-going part of our nature. In a man it is the conscious, in a woman, the unconscious. The Sun is warm, dry and vibrant.

THE MOON represents our needs. She rules the emotions, instincts, needs and feelings. She governs the feminine receptive part of our nature. In a woman she is the conscious, in a man, the unconscious. She is cool, wet and receptive.

MERCURY represents what we think and how we express our thoughts. He rules the intellect, the mind, written or spoken words, communication and travel. He is light, swift and bubbly.

VENUS represents our sense of beauty and our ability to love. She rules the esthetics, love and love affairs, music, painting and other arts. She is sensual, soft and gentle.

MARS represents our impulses and our ability to get what we want. He rules basic drives like sex and anger. He helps us in affirming ourselves. He is aggressive, daring and virile.

JUPITER represents our ability to expand. He governs truth, knowledge, religion, higher education, philosophy, law, enthusiasm, fortune, success and excess. He is lucky, exalted and jovial.

SATURN represents the structures and limitations in our lives. He rules the material world, self-preservation, contraction, stability, parents, authority figures and time. He is rigid, serious and organized.

URANUS represents our mental understanding of higher consciousness. He brings sudden changes, discoveries, revolutions, brotherhood, urge for freedom. He is individualistic, eccentric and unpredictable.

NEPTUNE represents the mystical longing to be at one with the universe. He touches the spiritual realms with the renunciation of the self. He rules creative aspirations, dissolution of boundaries, drugs, alcoholism and escapism. He is nebulous, immaterial and compassionate.

THE SUN	☉	♃	JUPITER
THE MOON	☽	♄	SATURN
MERCURY	☿	♅	URANUS
VENUS	♀	♆	NEPTUNE
MARS	♂	♇	PLUTO

PLUTO represents our selftransformation. He rules birth and death. In the underworld he causes feelings of guilt, revenge and helplessness with power control and manipulative tendencies, bringing with it the urge to transform ourselves. In a higher plane of consciousness Pluto gives rise to creativity, profound understanding and freedom of oneself and others. He is the phoenix who rises from the ashes.

THE ASPECTS

The aspects are the angles, measured in Zodiacal degrees, formed between planets or by a planet, and an important point in the chart. An orb is the range of influence around an aspect. When the Sun or the Moon is involved, two degrees more are allowed. The range of influence between a natal planet and a transiting planet is only of two degrees.

A CONJUNCTION occurs when two planets are within eight degrees of one another (within two degrees in a transit). It is the most powerful and intense interaction between two energies. In a transit it indicates the beginning of a new cycle of life, a total change or the results of one's effort coming to fruition.

A SEXTILE occurs when two planets form an angle of 60 degrees. This interaction offers opportunities, openings and ideas. It affects our immediate surroundings and our inner self. In a transit, changes require little effort.

A SQUARE occurs when two planets form an angle of 90 degrees. It is the most difficult and stressful aspect. The square provokes us into making necessary improvements in life. It forces us to make a further step into ourselves and the way we relate to others.

A TRINE occurs when two planets form an angle of 120 degrees. It is easy flowing and harmonious. In a transit things will go smoothly and without any effort. It is a time for expansion.

AN OPPOSITION occurs when two planets form an angle of 180 degrees. In this aspect, the two planets are over-stimulating each other and creating conflicts. Difficulty in personal relationships.

THE PHASES OF THE MOON

THE NEW MOON is when the Sun and the Moon are in conjunction – in the same place in the sky. The New Moon rises and sets with the Sun. It is visible a few days after the New Moon, towards the end of the first quarter, following the Sun as it sets. During the Waxing Moon our energies go from inside out, it is a time for new beginnings, relating and creativity.

THE SECOND QUARTER is when the Sun and the Moon square each other – when they form a 90 degree angle. This half crescent rises around noon and sets around midnight. It can be seen in the evening.

THE FULL MOON is when the Sun and the Moon are in opposites –

ARIES	♈	♎	LIBRA
TAURUS	♉	♏	SCORPIO
GEMINI	♊	♐	SAGITTARIUS
CANCER	♋	♑	CAPRICORN
LEO	♌	♒	ACQUARIUS
VIRGO	♍	♓	PISCES

when they form an 180 degrees angle. The Full Moon rises around sunset and sets around sunrise. It can be seen rising later every night during the third quarter. During the Waning Moon our energies go from outside in, it is a time for meditation and confrontation with oneself.

THE FOURTH QUARTER is when the Sun and the Moon square each other – when they form a 90 degree angle. This half crescent rises around midnight and sets around noon. It can be seen in the later part of the night.

ECLIPSES

THE SUN ECLIPSE occurs when the Moon is between the Sun and the Earth and only during the New Moon. The Moon passes in front of the Sun and acts as a curtain, hiding from us the rays of the Sun. The Sun eclipses, when they are total, are only visible in an area of 145km wide on the surface of the Earth. A PARTIAL eclipse is when the Moon doesn't com-

pletely cover the solar disk. A TOTAL eclipse is when the Moon completely covers the solar disk. An ANNULAR eclipse is like a total eclipse but the Moon is farther from the Earth and therefore the Moon will not entirely hide the Sun. A narrow ring of light will surround the dark New Moon.

THE MOON ECLIPSE occurs when the Earth is between the Sun and the Moon, projecting its shadow on the Moon. It only occurs during the Full Moon and is visible to the whole hemisphere turned towards it at that time. A PENUMBRAL eclipse is when the Moon enters only the penumbra of the Earth. A PARTIAL eclipse is when the Moon enters the Earth's shadow on the side opposite to the sun, without being totally immersed in it. A TOTAL eclipse is when the Moon is entirely immersed with the umbra.

THE MOON VOID OF COURSE

Just before the Moon enters a new sign, she will form a last major aspect with a planet. This time is called Void of Course. It has been observed that during the Void period, decision making is difficult, or unsuccessful, and if we do make a decision during that time, the results turn out to be different from our expectations. So don't make any decisions during those times and carry on as usual until the Void period finishes.

Since this phenomena is so important for our daily lives we have given the times of its occurrence. Next to the end of the Void period's time is the sign into which the Moon enters, these can help you to calculate the Moon transits. Check everyday if you don't want disappointing surprises.

NOTE: For all figures given in this datebook, check a time table to see what your time zone is compared to Greenwich Mean Time given in this book. For example if you are in Australia you would need to add eight to ten hours, if you are in U.S.A. five to eight. For the U.K. the time is the same.

JANUARY

*Before long everything
will be organized
We await a very evil century:
The lot of the masked and solitary
one (Clergy) greatly changed,
Few will be found who wish
to stay in their places.*

CAPRICORN
December 21st – January 19th
Cardinal – Earth
Negative – Extrapersonal
Rules the 10th House
Ruled by Saturn

As winter starts, the sun enters the sign of Capricorn – conserving, economical and restoring. If you are born under this sign you are concerned with the past. Ruled by Saturn, and by the element earth, your strict discipline makes you cold, distant, serious, avaricious and pessimistic. You will not deviate to the left or to the right, no matter what the obstacles and distractions are, self-denying in the process. Self-centered, you can be cold and insensitive to the needs of others. Yet you stick to your duty and will sacrifice yourself for it.

Diplomacy and tact are hiding a tough and persistent personality. A Capricorn can go through many frustrations, disappointments and failures keeping his calm, and graceful manners. You are prudent and don't easily open to others. You are reserved and cautious in expressing emotions. In romance you are quite demanding, but you won't let your emotions rule your understanding of the facts.

Conservative and traditional, you don't like extravagance and exhibitionism. You are just and to the point. Neat, tidy and practical you are an excellent organizer. To

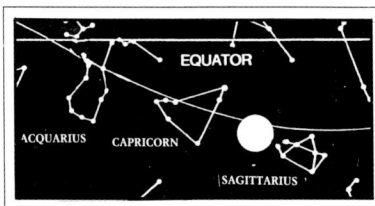

EQUATOR

ACQUARIUS   CAPRICORN

SAGITTARIUS

waste time and material is a crime to you. You are careful with money and expect others to give it its exact value.

Being of the element Earth you are not idealist, visionary or inventive, you rather take what is already there and improve or organize it. You also have a fine ability for investigation and research.

You plod along, but firm to the goal. Like the goat climbing the rocky mountains, you will climb the social ladder. Starting with nothing, you will struggle through the long and arduous journey to the top. You will find yourself among the great financiers, managers, lawyers and bankers. Your occupation can also be as researcher, real-estate agent, broker and farmer.

Once the soul has fulfilled its task in building structures and its roots are deep into the ground, the moment comes to discover the boundless horizons of the Aquarius. The deeper the roots, the higher the tree can be. The Capricorn has the roots and yet needs to learn about the freedom from the matter and spirit of his following Sun sign.

THE HEALING PROPHET

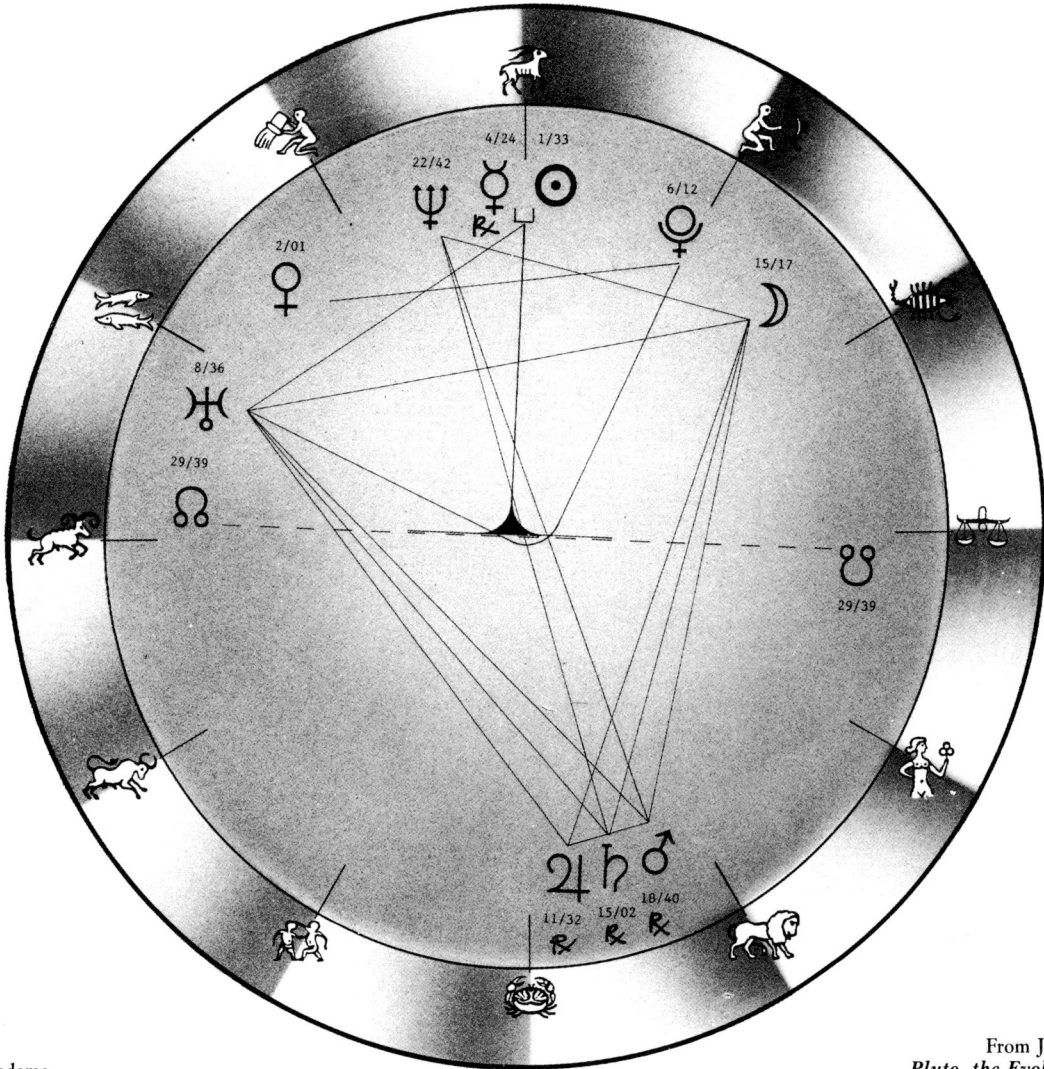

Michel
de Nostredame
December 14th, 1503, 12:03 p.m.

From Jeff Green
Pluto, the Evolutionary
Journey of the Soul Vol. I, 1986

NOSTRADAMUS BELIEVED that his gift of "sight" had a divine origin – that God gave him the power to see into the future. Within our own modern understanding of God as a part of each of our lives, this belief was of course correct – the source of his powers was his own clarity and his own divinity. It is also clear that Nostradamus believed in meditation for he spoke often of the problems of a "chattering mind" and how this constant talk within his mind often made the trance states he employed difficult to achieve. It has somehow, today, become evident to those involved in New Age philosophies, that any form of trance or deep meditation benefits from an ability to clear the mind of thoughts and the debris of modern life. It may well be that Nostradamus' gifts derived largely from a natural affinity with meditation and trance states which would, at that time, have been associated with religious beliefs.

Many of today's Masters such as Bhagwan Shree Rajneesh, Krishnamurti and Da Free John have spoken extensively on the deep strength that can be found in the peace of meditation and perhaps we may all come closer to prophecy through these methods during the next century.

The other factor that gave Nostradamus problems was the expression of his prophecies, for so much that comes from trance and meditation is impossible to express in words and it may well be that his extraordinarily complex forms of expression, with several languages, riddles and verses, arose out of a need to vary language to the maximum extent. It may also be why we, in the 20th century, have so much difficulty in deciphering what he said – for our language is purely in the mind.

The lady left alone in the realm
Her unique (husband) first
extinguished on the bed of honor:
For seven years she will
weep with grief
Then a long life and good fortune
for the kingdom.

CAPRICORN
Mars in exaltation
Mercury strong
Moon in detriment
Jupiter in fall

1 MONDAY

Moon Void of Course:
from 0:00 to 6:10 ♓

2 TUESDAY

3 WEDNESDAY

Moon Void of Course:
from 2:11 to 10:56 ♈

4 THURSDAY

10:40 ◑ 13 ♈ 49

5 FRIDAY

Moon Void of Course:
from 2:50 to 14:04 ♉

6 SATURDAY

The coffin is put in a vault of iron
Where seven children of the king
are held
Their ancestors will rise from
the depths of hell
Lamenting to see the fruits
of their line dead.

CAPRICORN
Stone: Turquoise
Metal: Lead
Color: Gray and brown
Animal: Mole, Goat
Bird: Vulture
Fish: Eel
Plant: Yew

7 SUNDAY

Moon Void of Course:
from 1:24 to 16:02 ♓

☉ 16 ♑ 25
☿ 21 ♑ 15 ℞
♀ 4 ♒ 53 ℞
♂ 13 ♐ 53
♃ 4 ♋ 25 ℞
♄ 16 ♑ 19
♅ 6 ♑ 7
♆ 12 ♑ 15
♇ 17 ♏ 14

8 MONDAY

Moon Void of Course:
from 17:01 to 24:00

9 TUESDAY

Moon Void of Course:
from 0:00 to 17:52 ♋

10 WEDNESDAY

11 THURSDAY

4:57 ○ 20 ♋ 42

Moon Void of Course:
from 4:57 to 21:02 ♌

12 FRIDAY

13 SATURDAY

Moon Void of Course:
from 5:31 to 24:00

The first son, a widow,
an unfortunate marriage
without any children.
Two islands plunged into discord:
Before eighteen years, still a minor,
For the other one betrothal happens
while even younger.

CAPRICORN
Rules knees, bones and skin
Identity: The Governor
Keyword: Ambition
Keynote: I utilize

14 SUNDAY

Moon Void of Course:
from 0:00 to 2:57 ♍

☉ 23 ♑ 33
☿ 12 ♑ 36 ℞
♀ 1 ♒ 34 ℞
♂ 18 ♐ 51
♃ 3 ♋ 33 ℞
♄ 17 ♑ 8
♅ 6 ♑ 32
♆ 12 ♑ 31
♇ 17 ♏ 24

15 MONDAY

16 TUESDAY

Moon Void of Course:
from 3:59 to 12:17 ♎

17 WEDNESDAY

18 THURSDAY

21:17 ◑ 28 ♎ 32

Moon Void of Course:
from 21:28 to 24:00

19 FRIDAY

Moon Void of Course:
from 0:00 to 0:16 ♏

20 SATURDAY

THE POPE SIXTUS PROPHECY

On a muddy road in Italy, not far from the town of Ancona, a group of Franciscan monks chanced upon the solitary doctor heading in the other direction. As he stood aside to let them pass he saw Brother Felice Peretti and immediately bowed, kneeling in the mud. The other friars were puzzled. Peretti was of low birth and the Lord had only delivered him from the pig sty a short while ago. They asked Nostradamus to explain, to which he replied, "I must yield myself and bend a knee before his Holiness." The friars thought this a joke but forty years after the incident Brother Peretti, the lowly born swine herder, became Pope Sixtus V, nineteen years after the death of Nostradamus.

There can be little doubt that aside from his extraordinary powers as a prophet, Nostradamus was equally gifted as a doctor. It seems that his abilities were partly associated with knowledge and understanding of medicine, but much more derived from a clear intelligence and a "calm spirit", abilities which may well have been lacking in others of his colleagues. Indeed, the prophet is not exactly complimentary about those he studied and worked with, calling their random methods, mostly using leeches, barbaric and uncivilized.

Nostradamus employed natural cures and cleanliness in his sometimes miraculous cures of the plague ridden countryside. Whether this derived from his view of the future or simply from a bright intelligence, is hard to be sure of. Perhaps it was a combination of the two, for there is no doubt that some of his cures were based on matters which would have been hard to know except by access to the future.

But in the main, the use of rose petals to give extra vitamin C placed under the tongue to provide a slow ingestion, is a very natural method which may have been around for centuries. Because we have rediscovered such cures within homeopathic studies of medicine does not mean we are the first to do so. Nostradamus probably did not understand the concept of vitamins in the way that we do, but the effect was the same.

The years spent traveling around the French rural areas were also a great risk to his own health and no doubt he would have employed many of his cures to save himself from the risks of the dreaded plague. These natural cures would certainly have presented him in a better light to his patients than the normal visiting doctors of the time, who would stuff garlic in their mouths and noses and arrive on the scene of the plague looking like something from outer space!

The application of clean water, clean air and the rose pills, together with the doctor's pleasant and bright presence, cured huge areas of France from a dangerously threatening plague.

NOSTRADAMUS' MEDICAL CURES

Rosehip

Lign Aloes

Odorated Calamus

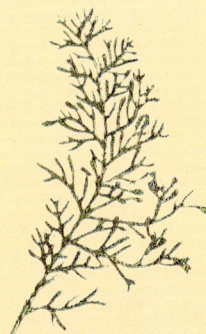

Green Cyprus

Iris of Florence

Clove

Nostradamus may have been aware of germs and the importance of sanitation through visions of the future. He would name Louis Pasteur in his writings hundreds of years before the great 19th century medical pioneer of micro-biology and vaccination was born.

Nostradamus would begin work on a plague stricken city such as Aix by first having all the corpses removed and the streets cleaned.

He could be found before sunrise in the fields outside town plucking roses by the hundreds, to be carried back to his makeshift pharmacy. He would dry and crush the rose petals into a fine powder, mixing them with a recipe of:

> *Sawd1st from green cyprus - 1 oz.*
> *Iris of Florence - 6 oz.*
> *Cloves - 3 oz.*
> *Odorated calamus - 3 drams*
> *Lign-aloes - 6 drams*

This concoction was packed tightly into lozenges he called "rose pills." He admonished his patients to keep these pills under their tongues at all times without swallowing them. Bleeding his patients was avoided. Clean water, bedding and air along with careful diet low on animal fat and moderate exercise helped most of his patients reponsd to the rose pills' strong does of vitamin C. These "rose pills" successfully cured the cities of Aix and Salon.

I sit at night alone in secret study
Resting upon the brass tripod:
A thin flame comes forth
from the solitude
Making successful
that which should not be
believed in vain.

AQUARIUS
January 20th – February 18th
Fixed – Air
Positive – Extrapersonal
Rules the 11th House
Ruled by Uranus

SUNDAY

21

Moon Void of Course:
from 7:02 to 12:44 ♐

☉	0 ♒ 41
☿	9 ♑ 45
♀	27 ♑ 20 ℞
♂	23 ♐ 50
♃	2 ♋ 45 ℞
♄	17 ♑ 58
♅	6 ♑ 56
♆	12 ♑ 46
♇	17 ♏ 32

22 **MONDAY**

23 **TUESDAY**

Moon Void of Course:
from 15:14 to 23:27 ♑

24 WEDNESDAY

25 THURSDAY

Moon Void of Course:
from 21:29 to 24:00

26 FRIDAY

19:20 ● 6 ≈ 35
18:53 Annular
solar eclipse
Moon Void of Course:
from 0:00 to 7:25 ≈

27 SATURDAY

28 SUNDAY

Moon Void of Course:
from 11:27 to 12:51 ♓

⊙ 7 ♒ 48
☿ 13 ♑ 7
♀ 23 ♑ 33 ℞
♂ 28 ♐ 51
♃ 2 ♋ 4 ℞
♄ 18 ♑ 46
♅ 7 ♑ 19
♆ 13 ♑ 1
♇ 17 ♏ 38

29 MONDAY

30 TUESDAY

Moon Void of Course:
from 4:01 to 16:34 ♈

31 WEDNESDAY

"Le Charbon" or the pestilence, that killed thousands in Nostradamus' time.

Nostradamus must have been aware of how disease would touch man in the future – perhaps he saw cancer and AIDS. His view, though, was influenced by the terminology and medical references of his own time.

"...Then the impurities and abominations will be brought to the surface and made manifest...towards the end of a change in reign (perhaps when Elizabeth gives way to Charles)...in the meantime (there appears) so vast a plague that two thirds of the world will fail and decay. So many (die) that no one will know the true owners of fields and houses. The weeds in the streets will rise higher than the knees, and there shall be a total desolation of the Clergy."

Predictions made today, about the potential power of AIDS to devastate population run close to the predictions made by Nostradamus – already we can see that there are potentially over a hundred million people who may be AIDS positive in the United States alone. The last remark in this piece of the *Epistle* from the Prophet to Henry II of France, is perhaps one of the most significant – that the Clergy will be in "total desolation", for it is now suggested that much of the AIDS virus is striking within the Church.

Nostradamus was even closer in his prediction that "...relief near, but remedy far away." In relation to AIDS cure progress, methods have been discovered to postpone the actual death of AIDS sufferers in the form of drugs named *suramin* and *ribavarin* and we see in one of the quatrains some-

thing that has puzzled experts for years. The word *Samarobrin* which forms a fascinating combination of the two names. But still today, there is no cure for this awesome disease – and if the Prophet's words are correct we may have to wait a lot longer for any cure.

If the growth of the disease continues at its present rate, there will be two hundred million people dead from AIDS by the late 1990s in the US alone where the total population is likely to be only three hundred million plus – that's two-thirds.

FEBRUARY

The great city of the maritime ocean,
Surrounded by a swamp of crystal:
In the winter solstice and the spring
Will be tried by a terrible wind.

AQUARIUS
Neptune in exaltation
Venus strong
Sun in detriment
Pluto in fall

If you are born as the sun travels in Aquarius you have inherited the strong-will and intellectual character of this airy and fixed sign. Although reserved, kind, naive and frivolous at times, you enjoy shocking more conventional people. Usually a refined individual you can suddenly come up with the most amazing statements and actions at the most unpredictable times. They are in for surprises who join the company of your eccentric soul.

Ruled by Uranus, you own a great understanding for humanity and hate cruelty of any kind. Everybody is your "brother", but you won't have many intimate friends. You possess a natural ability to read the characters of others, which can turn into disappointment in people as you see their faults. The humanitarian can turn selfish, false and egoist, wanting to be alone and resenting it if

anyone offers their help or interferes in any way.

Being of the element Air you are intuitive, idealistic and intellectual. You have the ability to transcend the material and look beyond it. You are electrifying, magnetic, explosive, quick and ac-

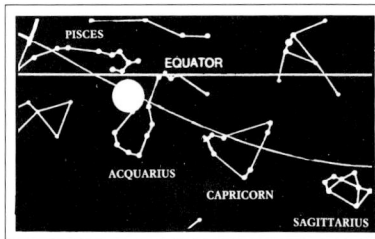

tive, always in a state of internal unrest. You don't like to be confined to one spot. You hate structures, routine work or fixed plans for the future and will rebel against any strict rules set upon you.

In romance you need intellectual stimulation. You can become

very sweetly romantic, but your attention doesn't last for long: a new intellectual adventure and you are gone. You prefer to care about the whole of humanity rather than about a family and close ones.

If there is a challenge, you tend to overwork, being capable of resisting fatigue, and in this way often injuring your health. You will make a good literary worker, scientific worker, genius, post-office and telegraph employee, surveyor, engineer, astronomer and astrologer.

In the Aquarius the soul feels like a free spirit, equal to all humans. It has reached boundless skies and is now ready to melt into the universe. The completion of the soul is found in the Sun sign of Pisces, completing the Zodiac with its last sign. There the Aquarius will learn about compassion, how to care for others and how to share his genius.

CAPTAINS AND KINGS

What may have been some form of solar light in the skies of Paris, the "Mercure Français" of 1619 describes an army of armed ghosts parading in their thousands on the eve of Henry IV's assassination.

ERHAPS ONE OF THE MOST bizarre aspects of any form of prediction is that it may influence the times it speaks of. In a way we enter the realms of science fiction, of time travel, when we speak of someone changing the future from the past – the present time, if influenced by past predictions, then clearly changes it own future.

Within his own time it is clear that Nostradamus influenced events strongly when he advised members of the French Royal House of how their fate would unfold, to the extent of altering whole lines of the Royal Family, but perhaps we are even today influenced enough by his words to make changes that we would not otherwise make.

Certainly those who pay close attention to his astrological workings could not deny that our future has always been written in the stars and it is purely a matter of how well we interpret it, whether or not we can change it too.

But most of the time we do not listen, either to warnings of the past or of the present, for we are so busy trying to alter our own lives that we have little time to look at the life of the planet.

Masters and gurus of the past have been warning us of the fates we will confront during the latter part of this century, for thousands of years and very little has been done to pay attention to these warnings.

And most of them say the same things – that unless we alter and raise our global level of consciousness there is very little hope of ever getting much past the end of this millennium.

Perhaps the strongest message from Nostradamus was exactly this – that with all the doom and disaster he predicted, there was still one way out – through a higher consciousness of our potential and our surroundings.

If we have listened to him at all, we have listened to the fear his predictions engender in us and perhaps these forceful warnings will help us influence our own future, from his view of it.

During the summer of 1565 two medical students traveled from Bordeaux to Salon to tell the Prophet what they thought of his predictions – "You have done incredible damage with your prophecies. People can no longer sleep. They sell their belongings and spend their last savings because they no longer believe it worthwhile to make plans for the future. We have even heard stories of a

few people so vexed by your prophecies that they killed themselves rather than wait for the fulfillment of them. Can you not repent and take responsibility for all the damage you have done?"

Nostradamus replied – "Well, my friends, you think it is irresponsible, and even criminal to look into the future and pronounce loudly what will happen to us. Why? Our Lord Jesus Christ has also talked openly about the fall of Jerusalem, Solomon's Temple, and how the world will be destroyed one day, and always he proclaimed that the prophets have said the same before... I know I have but one year left to live. Every man is absolutely certain his life will end in a catastrophe, namely death. Is this a reason to give up and wail, or even kill oneself because one day, sooner or later, everything will end with death?"

"But you have spread great fear," countered the students.

"When people are desperate out of fear, then the doctor's job is to fight that fear and help them get strong. It alone is the cause of all damage. And fear comes foremost from unfulfilled desires. The one who tells people that life need have no cares and is nothing but "jolly" is worse than the prophet. When you become doctors you will encounter it. Fear is the door. Through it comes all sickness. It creates war and all other activities. Fear makes plagues and illusions. Only fear. It is always so. My prophecies do not spread fear. I am the writer of future history. The one who is reasonable can learn from my prophecies how to find the right path to take as if he would have found footprints in the sand from someone who has gone before. Study the history of ancient cultures. The ancient peoples have left behind witnesses of inner silence, radiance, benediction and beauty and the nations of the future will only pass on traces of plague and death."

Certainly in this last prophecy he was right, for we have not gained nations in the future that he saw, that seem any the wiser than they ever were during his time.

The "Captains and Kings"

The tournament in which King Henry II was fatally wounded, 1559.

Nostradamus and Catharine de' Medici together performed what in their time would have been a pagan rite of divination, absolutely in contradiction to the laws of the Inquisition.

that we have employed to administer and guide our nations seem very often little better than strange actors on a stranger stage – constantly in trouble, constantly at war, constantly unable to make any serious impression on the world they have inherited.

Nostradamus had enough trouble guiding the royalty of his own times – what trouble would he have had with characters such as Khomeini, Khaddafi, Abu Nidal and Abu Abbas, the potential "Anti-Christs" of today.

In of of his most famous sets of predictions the prophet pointed to a future dominated by three anti-christs. The first two are already well know to us – Napoleon and Hitler and these two he named directly.

How a single man in the 16th century could possibly pick out actual names from reading the stars remains an astonishing miracle. But this he did. And he went still further in stating that there would be a third anti-christ who would dominate the end of the 20th century.

"The third anti-christ very soon annihilated.
Twenty-seven years his bloody war will last:
The heretics are dead, captives, exiled
Blood soaked human bodies, water and a reddened icy rain covering the entire earth."

Sadly, as often is the case, it is hard to pin-point exactly the character Nostradamus was pointing to, unless of course it wasn't simply one person to whom he referred.

Interpreters of Nostradamus' works have come round increasingly to propose that he spoke of a series of groups or people who dominate our lives today – namely those who have perpetrated the terrifying horrors of revolutionary activity during the past years.

Some interpretation imply that Nostradamus would have seen us as being perpetually at war during the twenty-seven years from the beginning of the "Six-day War" bringing the end neatly to coincide with the end of this millennium. Perhaps, then, the third world war is now in progress – it would certainly seem so, viewed from the 1500s.

But how have his predictions worked out in these last few years since *Nostradamus and the Millennium* was first published. Perhaps we can look in some detail at those concerned with the "Captains and

More a butcher than a King
of England
Born of obscure rank he will gain
Empire through force.
A coward without faith, without law,
he will bleed the land.
His time approaches so near
that I sigh.

AQUARIUS
Stone: Amethyst
Metal: Lead
Color: Electric blue

1

THURSDAY

Moon Void of Course:
from 5:52 to 19:27 ☿

2

FRIDAY

18:32 ◐ **13** ☿ **40**

3

SATURDAY

Moon Void of Course:
from 7:43 to 22:12 ♓

In the head of Aries (lies) Jupiter
and Saturn.
Eternal God what changes!
Then the bad times return after
a long century,
What turmoil in France and Italy.

AQUARIUS
Animal: Jackal
Bird: Vulture
Fish: Cuttlefish
Plant: Beech

---

4 SUNDAY

☉ 14 ≈ 54
☿ 19 ♑ 57
♀ 21 ♑ 19 ℞
♂ 3 ♑ 54
♃ 1 ♋ 31 ℞
♄ 19 ♑ 33
♅ 7 ♑ 41
♆ 13 ♑ 16
♇ 17 ♏ 43

---

5 MONDAY

Moon Void of Course:
from 1:24 to 24:00

---

6 TUESDAY

Moon Void of Course:
from 0:00 to 1:27 ♋

7

WEDNESDAY

Moon Void of Course:
from 20:10 to 24:00

8

THURSDAY

Moon Void of Course:
from 0:00 to 5:51 ♌

9

FRIDAY

19:16 ○ 20 ♌ 47
19:12 Total lunar eclipse

Moon Void of Course:
from 19:16 to 24:00

10

SATURDAY

Moon Void of Course:
from 0:00 to 12:13 ♍

*The walls will change from brick
to marble.
Fifty-seven peaceful years:
Joy to humans, the aqueduct renewed,
Health, abundant fruit,
mellifluous times.*

AQUARIUS
Rules ankles
Identity: The Innovator
Keyword: Truth
Keynote: I know

11 SUNDAY

☉	22 ♒	0
☿	28 ♑	36
♀	21 ♑	4
♂	8 ♑	59
♃	1 ♋	8 ℞
♄	20 ♑	19
♅	8 ♑	1
♆	13 ♑	29
♇	17 ♏	46

12 MONDAY

Moon Void of Course:
from 4:11 to 21:09 ♎

13 TUESDAY

14 WEDNESDAY

15 THURSDAY

Moon Void of Course:
from 0:40 to 8:34 ♏

16 FRIDAY

17 SATURDAY

18:48 ◑ 28 ♏ 51

Moon Void of Course:
from 18:48 to 21:07 ♐

The blood of the just will be
demanded of London,
Burnt by fire in the year'66.
The ancient lady will fall
from her high place.
And many of the same sect
will be killed.

PISCES
February 19th – March 20th
Mutable – Water
Negative – Extrapersonal
Rules the 12th House
Ruled by Neptune

18 SUNDAY

Moon Void of Course:
from 15:50 to 24:00

☉	29	♒	4
☿	8	♒	22
♀	22	♑	41
♂	14	♑	5
♃	0	♋	53 ℞
♄	21	♑	3
♅	8	♑	20
♆	13	♑	42
♇	17	♏	47

19 MONDAY

Moon Void of Course:
from 0:00 to 24:00

20 TUESDAY

Moon Void of Course:
from 0:00 to 8:30 ♑

21
WEDNESDAY

22
THURSDAY

Moon Void of Course:
from 6:42 to 16:52 ≈

23
FRIDAY

24
SATURDAY

Moon Void of Course:
from 0:38 to 21:49 ⅹ

25 SUNDAY

8:54 ● 6 ♓ 30

☉	6 ♓	7
☿	19 ♒	1
♀	25 ♉	50
♂	19 ♉	12
♃	0 ♋	49
♄	21 ♉	45
♅	8 ♉	38
♆	13 ♉	54
♇	17 ♏	47 ℞

26 MONDAY

Moon Void of Course:
from 19:03 to 24:00

27 TUESDAY

Moon Void of Course:
from 0:00 to 0:16 ♈

28 WEDNESDAY

Moon Void of Course:
from 22:41 to 24:00

Nostradamus accurately predicts the year of the Great Fire of London in 1666.

Kings" of the years 1986 – 1989.
"The communal law will be made in opposition.
The old order will hold strong, then are removed from the scene:
Then Communism put far behind."
and
"The law of More will be seen to decline,
Followed by one more pleasing."
In the diary at the back of *Nostradamus and the Millennium* these two quatrains were quoted as being significant in terms of the changes to take place in Communist Russia. The reference to "More" is Sir Thomas More, the author of *Utopia* who laid down the very first Communist Manifesto.

The quatrains' main thrust is to predict that the Communist world will change during the latter part of the 20th century and the interpretation was made shortly before Gorbachev announced his "Glasnost" clean out of the old Communist ways, bringing a "more pleasing" order towards the end of the century – exactly as predicted.

According to the following quatrain, we shall see a US-Soviet Alliance:
"One day the great powers will become friends
Their great power will be seen to increase.
The new land (America) will be at the height of its power.
To the man of blood the number is reported."

The closer we have come to this year, the closer it seems the US and the Soviet Union have come together.

It remains to be seen whether any treaty is made between the two great super-powers before 1990 itself. It will be most interesting to find out if the "man of blood" referred to in the quatrain has any basis in reality.

Of course, Nostradamus was long experienced at looking forward to the rise and fall of various empires of the future. He foresaw

Austria's rise and collapse, the rise of the United States and its collapse and in earlier times the rise and fall of the British Empire.

As shown on these pages, the tracing of the rapid increase in power and wealth in England was seen by the prophet through the the story of royalty, once again. In one short quatrain he summed up the whole change:
"Seven times you will see the British nation change,
Dyed (stained) in blood for two hundred and ninety years.
Not at all free from Germania's influence,
Aries doubts the protector of Poland."

In seven heads of state spanning two hundred and ninety years, we see the exact fulfillment of the prophet's words – from Elizabeth I through Cromwell, the two Charles, Queen Anne, George I and finally Hitler – whose threat against England was epitomized by her need to be "the protector of Poland" – the British Empire reached its zenith in the domination of the world and then fell sharply to its death after the incredible cost of the Second World War. And it is not as though Nostradamus predicted three centuries but exactly two hundred and ninety years.

His interest in power and gov-

The fortress near the Thames will fall
When the King is locked up inside,
He will be seen in his shirt near the bridge,
One confronting death then barred in the fort.

ernment is reflected throughout all the "Centuries" in which he made his verses and letters and there are still some mighty nations to fall that might seem now, to us of the 20th century, unlikely.

The next most significant time, of course, begins in the early 1990s – the years that will be covered by *The Nostradamus Astrological Date Books*.

Keep watching for more news!

ELISABETH I

The death of Elisabeth I brings extinction to the House of Tudor and brings James I and the House of Stuart to the english throne in 1603.

OLIVER CROMWELL

The english Civil War brings a more violent change in blood. The word "Taintz", used by the prophet, can mean "dyed", describing the famous british redcoats worn throughout the Empire years by the english soldiers, which were first seen on the backs of Cromwell's Army.

CHARLES II

Charles returns to the House of Stuart to the throne after Cromwell's dictatorship in 1660.

WILLIAM III

The glorious revolution of 1699 shuffles Stuarts out, in favor of William III of Friesland.

QUEEN ANNE

The House of Stuart returns with Queen Anne in 1702.

GEORGE I

German blue bloods take the throne warmed by Queen Anne with the arrival of George I and House of Hanover in 1714.

HITLER

Line four predicts the end of royal blood-power from a more malevolent German influence. It foretells the blood-bath of World War II set off by Hitler (Aries = God of War) not believing England's threat that they would go to war to protect Poland.

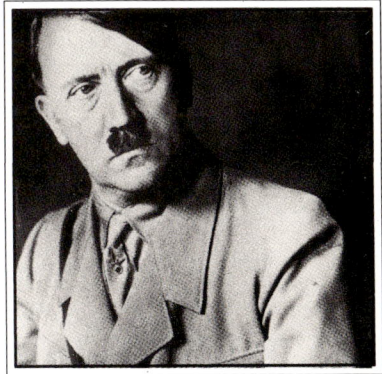

MARCH

A trembling of the Earth at Mortara,
The tin islands of
St. George half sunk:
Drowsy with peace, war will awaken,
The abyss of the temple
ripped open at Easter (spring).

PISCES
Venus in exaltation
Moon strong
Mercury in detriment
Mercury in fall

In the cold winter nature has slowed down, the leaves are gone from the trees, it is a time of rest and even sleep for a lot of animals. It seems that the ones born in the last month of winter have inherited Mother Nature's gifts. The most feminine of all signs, you are gentle, lazy, fun, sensitive and impressionable.

Aquatic, deceptive and delusive, you are not a struggler. You will give up your goal and dream how wonderful it would have been, rather than go through the obstacles and frustrations found on the way. You would rather go with the flow than fight against it. You tend to see the world in pink and you lack the "oomph" to be really ambitious.

Being the last sign of the Zodiac, you have retained the wisdom of all the other signs: your enthusiasm comes from Aries, your laziness from Taurus, your clever-ness from Gemini, your fun outgoing nature from Leo, your concentration on detail from Virgo, your love of pleasure and charm from Libra, your depth of character from Scorpio, your idealism from Sagittarius, your organizational ability from Capricorn and your mischeivousness from the Aquarius.

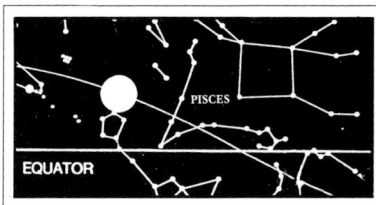

You also own the greatest task of the Zodiac: your natural connection to the unconscious and things of the "beyond" becomes a longing for mystical fulfillment and you often feel misunderstood by others. If your longing to be part of the greater whole is not fulfilled, it can sometimes lead you to drugs and alcoholism.

Anyone looking for a romantic, caring and tender partner, will find him in the Pisces. You are sensual, warm and sensitive, but you will need someone practical to make your dream come true.

Your unjudging nature loves everyone unconditionally. You love to help the sick and weak and if someone has an emotional problem you will give them tons of advice. You can also be found among the nurses and doctors or any place you can be of any use to others. Deeply sensitive, you love art, poetry and music. You can also be psychic and a medium. Your aquatic character can lead you into professions which have to do with liquids, like barman or sailor.

Going towards Aries, the Pisces has yet to acquire the courage and initiative of his following Sun sign.

SHADOW OF THE GUILLOTINE

NOSTRADAMUS POSSESSED a macabre sense of humor which perhaps arose out of his lack of fear of death. This is perhaps illustrated by the story of the medallion around his neck bearing the very date of 1700 when his body was exhumed by the Salon City Council. Ninety-one years later, the quatrain warning future desecrators of his grave of their impending death, also came to fulfillment, at least according to the stories told of the time.

Nostradamus probably relied strongly on people's natural superstition combined with the power of his reputation. It may be, according to recent para-psychological researches, that the human being has the power to fulfill fears that are sufficiently strong so that many of Nostradamus' predictions could unfold simply through a combination of this facility and the knowledge he possessed of human nature.

Very recent research into genetic evolutionary development suggests that we humans possess a DNA memory which works to record direct environmental experience *during* each lifetime.

Put another way, if we experience an event such as nuclear war, famine or occurrences of pollution in our environment, or even minor experiences such as city life, accidents or traumatic events, then all these experiences are recorded in the genetic system, not merely in a life-time's memory. They are therefore not lost at the time of death but passed on to the next generation.

The implications of this understanding, if proved to be true, are that we humans actually develop our own evolution completely. We are solely responsible for the way the future unfolds, not some greater power called God or Nature – us humans!

Perhaps Nostradamus had a direct knowledge of this aspect of human science – either through his "seeing" of the future or simply because he possessed a unique comprehension of human nature. In fact, such a comprehension would be basically the same thing as "seeing" the future.

In this respect, his knowledge of the future of the time he lived in would be exactly the same as that of the very far distant future, for human nature does not change to any great extent, unless perhaps influenced by alien races – something that Nostradamus did not specifically point at in our future. One aspect of his knowledge and that of our own present knowledge, which would be worth looking at, however, is the whole fascinating concept of time itself.

In the Western civilizations time is taken very much for granted and we tend to presume that we all exist in the same time. This is today being proved to be false. The Hopi Indians, for example, have a very different view of how time works, not having the words "past," "present," and "future" in their vocabulary at all. Their universe consists of what is "manifest" and what is about to be manifest and the present is a "razor's edge" between the two. Hopi children have no concept of our clock time but perceive rhythm, velocity and frequency as their connection with minutes and seconds. The Chinese writer and Master Hung Po stated: "Beginningless time and the present moment are the same. You have only to understand that time has no real existence." If we look at the human mind it appears to spend all of its time either in the past or the future, with very little concern for the present.

Perhaps the most interesting aspect of our historical "time-travel" has been that since we derived our understanding of time as a science we have become so preoccupied by it that history has

The execution of Marie-Antoinette.

Dronning af Frankerige Henrettelse den 16.October 1793.

The arrest of the royal family on their flight to Varennes.

been viewed only with the whole process of past through present into future. We even write our science fiction stories with the fundamental concept that we might one day manage to travel through time, either into the past or the future and look once again at history or sample what we may do one day hence.

The whole imaginative dabbling in time travel has given rise to some fascinating confusions. What, for example, happens when we travel back into a place in the past? We take our human body and we become part of a period of history which we have nothing to do with – we therefore inevitably influence that time with our presence – which means in turn that we

When the Bour' is very "bon"
Bearing in himself marks of justice
Then bearing the oldest name
of his blood:
Through flight he will unjustly
receive his punishment.

PISCES
Stone: Aquamarine
Metal: Tin
Color: Light turquoise

1

THURSDAY

Moon Void of Course:
from 0:00 to 1:43 ♀

2

FRIDAY

3

SATURDAY

Moon Void of Course:
from 2:55 to 3:37 ♓

*Coins depreciated by the spirit
of the kingdom
People will be stirred up
against their king.
New saints make peace,
holy laws become worse
Paris was never in such great trouble.*

PISCES
Animal: Elephant
Bird: Eagle
Fish: All fishes
Plant: Oak

4 SUNDAY

2:05 ◗ 13 ♓ 14

Moon Void of Course:
from 2:05 to 24:00

☉	13 ♓	9
☿	0 ♓	29
♀	0 ♒	11
♂	24 ♑	21
♃	0 ♋	54
♄	22 ♑	23
♅	8 ♑	53
♆	14 ♑	4
♇	17 ♏	44 ℞

5 MONDAY

Moon Void of Course:
from 0:00 to 7:02 ♋

6 TUESDAY

7

WEDNESDAY

Moon Void of Course:
from 6:33 to 12:24 ♌

8

THURSDAY

Moon Void of Course:
from 20:50 to 24:00

9

FRIDAY

Moon Void of Course:
from 0:00 to 19:47 ♍

10

SATURDAY

*By night he will come
by the forest of Reines
A married couple, devious route,
Queen white stone:
A monk-king in gray in Varennes
Elected Cap, caused tempest, fire,
and bloody slicing.*

PISCES
Rules the feet
Identity: The Dreamer
Keyword: Unity
Keynote: I imagine

---

11 SUNDAY

10:59 ○ 20 ♍ 37

Moon Void of Course:
from 15:39 to 24:00

☉	20 ♓	9
☿	12 ♓	48
♀	5 ♒	24
♂	29 ♑	31
♃	1 ♋	8
♄	22 ♑	59
♅	9 ♑	6
♆	14 ♑	13
♇	17 ♏	40 ℞

---

12 MONDAY

Moon Void of Course:
from 0:00 to 5:09 ♎

---

13 TUESDAY

14

WEDNESDAY

Moon Void of Course:
from 2:54 to 16:25 ♏

15

THURSDAY

16

FRIDAY

Moon Void of Course:
from 20:51 to 24:00

17

SATURDAY

Moon Void of Course:
from 0:00 to 4:56 ♐

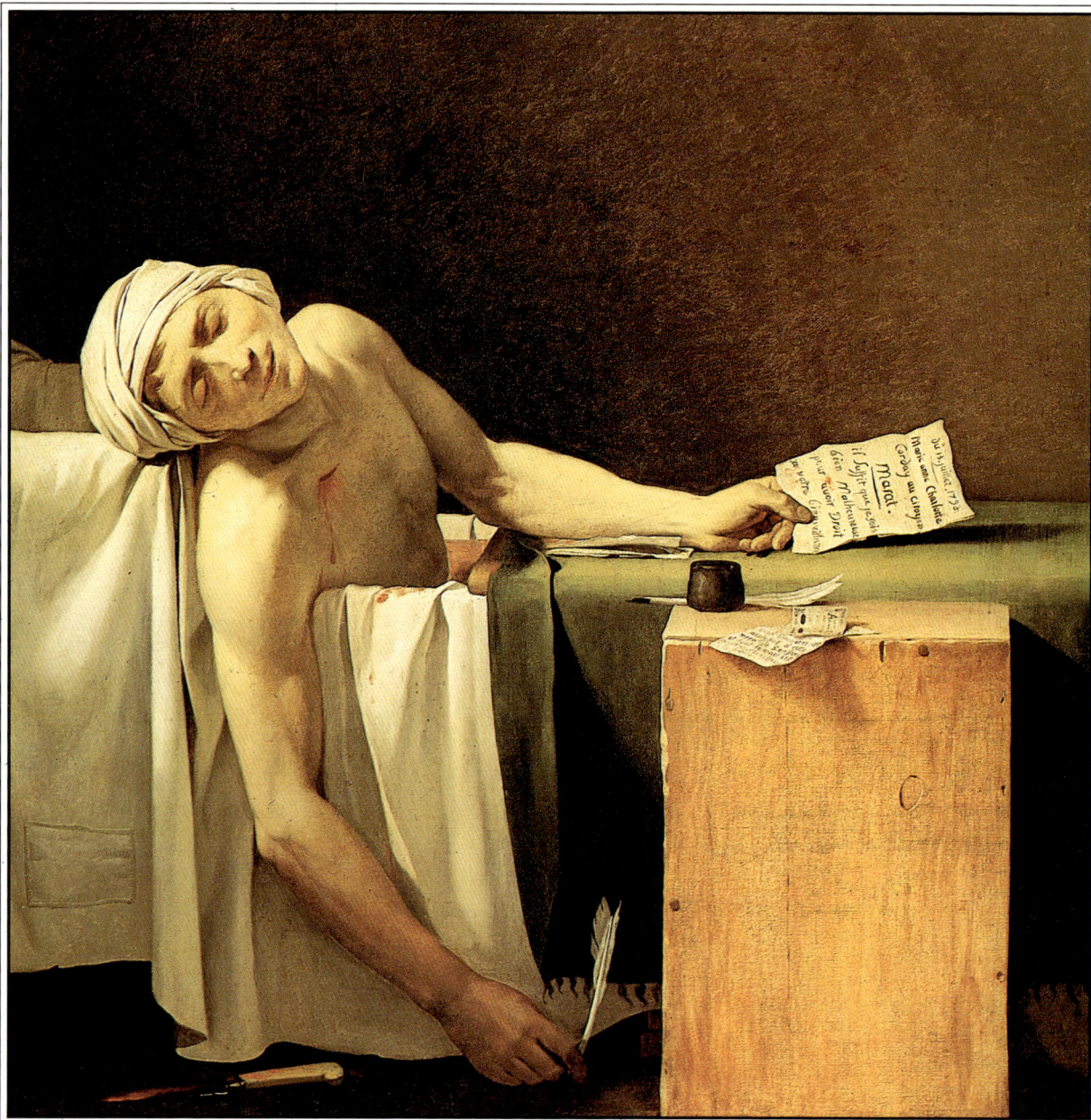

MARAT One of the "headless idiots" all murdered by the excess of their revolution.

Marie-Antoinette
with her children.

will influence the future of that time.

Various of the best known Science Fiction writers have supposed that if we behave in a particular fashion – in the past – we may manage to do something that actually prevents our being born in our own time – this kind of influence is rather like a vacuum cleaner sucking itself up! For if we have gone into the past and prevented something from happening there, which eventually results in our not being born, then how could we go back into the past in the first place – when we were never there!?

Such complexity can also be seen in the light of Nostradamus' influence on his own future. His predictions, as we have sampled, may cause us, about whom he wrote, to change our attitudes to life, thus, in a way, bringing the Prophet into his own future as a time traveler.

And as far as his reputation as a time traveler is concerned, his books continue to sell in their hundreds of thousands, *Nostradamus* *and the Millennium* being no exception. We love to see the future.

The content of this Date Book is evidence of this natural (or unnatural) human propensity and during the next "month" of the book we will look more closely at why we and Nostradamus have such a passion for time, in the hope that this may help us to understand the way he worked.

*The Queen sent to death
by jurors chosen by lot:
They will deny the Queen's son,
And the prostitute shares
the fate of the consort.*

ARIES
March 21st – April 19th
Cardinal – Fire
Positive – Personal
Rules the 1st House
Ruled by Mars

18 SUNDAY

☉	27 ♓	8
☿	26 ♓	3
♀	11 ♒	19
♂	4 ♒	42
♃	1 ♋	32
♄	23 ♑	31
♅	9 ♑	17
♆	14 ♑	20
♇	17 ♏	35 ℞

19 MONDAY

14:30 ☽ 28 ♐ 43

Moon Void of Course:
from 15:39 to 17:01 ♑

20 TUESDAY

21 WEDNESDAY

Moon Void of Course:
from 14:53 to 24:00

22 THURSDAY

Moon Void of Course:
from 0:00 to 2:31 ≈

23 FRIDAY

Moon Void of Course:
from 10:16 to 24:00

24 SATURDAY

Moon Void of Course:
from 0:00 to 8:09 ✕

*The premier citizen of
the city in revolt
Who will struggle hard
to regain their liberty:
The men are cut up, unhappy mixture,
Cries, howlings at Nantes,
piteous to see!*

ARIES
Sun in exaltation
Jupiter strong
Venus in detriment
Saturn in fall

☉	4 ♈	5
☿	10 ♈	3
♀	17 ♒	44
♂	9 ♒	54
♃	2 ♋	5
♄	24 ♉	0
♅	9 ♉	25
♆	14 ♉	26
♇	17 ♏	28 ℞

25 SUNDAY

26 MONDAY

19:48 ● 5 ♈ 53

Moon Void of Course:
from 0:33 to 10:15 ♈

27 TUESDAY

28 WEDNESDAY

Moon Void of Course:
from 1:09 to 10:26 ☿

29 THURSDAY

30 FRIDAY

Moon Void of Course:
from 1:26 to 10:42 ♓

31 SATURDAY

APRIL

ARIES
Stone: Diamond
Metal: Iron
Color: Red

The time will be filthy,
pestilent and violent,
A terrible Moslem attack and invasion.
Great disasters are made in April
And great persons will be ridiculed,
but for two of them.

Spring has come and life returns. The sprouts are pushing their way out, the leaves are growing and the flowers blossom. As nature gives birth again, your bubbly, fiery, impulsive, enthusiastic Aries nature is bursting with life and ideas. Nothing scares you. Always ready for something more, you speed along your path, courageously pushing away any obstacles in the way. You hate tedious jobs and will rarely finish what you have started, preferring the excitement of the new. Impatient and bad tempered at times, you can handle almost any tough situation, but when it comes to pain, your courage runs out.

Ruled by Mars you know where you stand and have a mind of your own. You are a leader and hate being pushed around or told what to do. When most negative, you are stubborn, aggressive and dominate others. You won't recognize a defeat and even though you are surrounded by a tough shell you are very sensitive and touchy. Extremely intuitive you can sense others to an extraordinary extent.

Proud and full of self-esteem, you love compliments and will expect tons of them from others. The passionate, jealous and possessive Aries is incapable of going half way, scrupulously faithful you will expect the same from your romantic partner and unless he makes you the center of attention and matches your ideals, he won't be able to keep hold of you.

Very impulsive, your emotions are let loose in a flash and you can readily become rude, bad tempered and even violent at times. But don't forget that the more positive side of this makes you enthusiastic and passionate.

Although frank, candid and naive, you don't always stick to truth and tend to exaggerate and magnify the facts. Loud in speech at times, inconsiderate of others you tend to go to extremes and over-stress yourself.

In a career you always need to improve yourself. You are fiery and ambitious, you will change occupations many times in your life, but you will always be either the boss in your work or involved in a profession of your choice, working independently or having your own business.

Through Aries the soul is born. Nothing will stop its ardor to plant new seeds along its path by bringing out ideas and starting new projects. But the Aries lacks the patience for finishing what he has started and therefore needs to learn those qualities well known from his following Sun sign, the Taurus.

CHILD OF THE GUILLOTINE

NAPOLEON BEFORE...

AND AFTER

OSTRADAMUS' "SIGHT", for example of Napoleon, was a truly extraordinary achievement, for which it is hard to account. It is not as if the prophet simply made vague indications of the man. He actually gave us his name! Admittedly he spelled it wrong, but we cannot fault the man for a small spelling error, especially considering how close it was – "Napaulon."

The events that surrounded the life of Napoleon are described by the prophet with such accuracy that there can be little doubt of his powers of perception and it is of great interest to examine how it may have been possible for Nostradamus to see what he did.

If we look at the modern philosophical understanding of time we see that the concept of past, present and future become somewhat of an illusion.

When we think of the past – something we did yesterday, it is not that we are then *in* the past, for our memory exists within the mind *now* not yesterday. And when we have expectations of the future, something that may happen tomorrow, we are having that expectation now, not tomorrow. The mind, therefore, is always in the present and cannot be anywhere else. Our perception of past and future is a mistake and relates only to the idea that there is a time span between past memory and present knowledge.

"Mind is always *now*. There is really no before and after for mind. There is only a *now* that includes memories and expectations." E. Schroedinger.

Once we begin to understand this very simple concept it becomes clearer that perhaps an appreciation of time as "all one" would make it possible for someone with a sufficiently keen intelligence and clear mind to see all events that occur, past, present and future.

If we look closely at space, for example, it becomes easily provable that all space is infinite – i.e. it exists everywhere – or – infinity is completely present at *every* point of the universe. And as infinity is to space so eternity is to time. All eternity – or all time – is completely present at every point in time. Thus from the point of view of eternity, all time is *now*, just as to

An Emperor will be born near Italy.
He will cost his empire very dearly;
They will say that from the sort of
people that surround him
He is less a prince than a butcher.

the infinite, all space is *here*. As all time is now, it follows that the past and future are illusions and the only reality is present reality.

If this all sounds a bit too philosophical it should be remembered how often we as individuals have "hunches" and experience such phenomena as "deja vu" or coincidence. These experiences, much recorded in areas of parapsychology, indicate the possibility that in our passion for the future, we forget that perhaps it is all happening right before our eyes!

And certainly it appears that it *was* all happening before the eyes of Nostradamus for one of his methods for divining the future was to enter a trance state using large doses of a natural potion derived from nutmeg, somewhat similar to modern chemical drugs in its effect. Nostradamus believed that the presence of nutmeg in large doses caused a clearing of the mental chatter associated with the diversions of past and future.

PAU, NAY, LORON will be more
of fire than of the blood,
To swim in praise, the great one
to flee to the confluence.
He will refuse entry to the Piuses,
The depraved ones and the Durance
(France) will keep them imprisoned.

ARIES
Animal: Wolf and sheep
Bird: Hawk
Fish: Pike
Plant: Pine

1 SUNDAY

Moon Void of Course:
from 3:48 to 12:50 ♋

☉ 11 ♈ 0
☿ 23 ♈ 57
♀ 24 ♒ 33
♂ 15 ♒ 7
♃ 2 ♋ 46
♄ 24 ♑ 25
♅ 9 ♑ 31
♆ 14 ♑ 31
♇ 17 ♏ 20

2 MONDAY

10:24 ◑ 12 ♋ 25

3 TUESDAY

Moon Void of Course:
from 15:44 to 17:50 ♌

4 WEDNESDAY

5 THURSDAY

6 FRIDAY

Moon Void of Course:
from 1:02 to 1:42 ♍

7 SATURDAY

> *Quite a different man will attain*
> *to great Empire.*
> *Distant from kindness,*
> *more so from happiness,*
> *Ruled by one coming a short time*
> *from his bed.*
> *The kingdom rushes towards*
> *great misfortune.*

ARIES
Rules the head
Identity: The Pioneer
Keyword: Action
Keynote: I am

8 SUNDAY

Moon Void of Course:
from 1:27 to 11:44 ♎

☉ 17 ♈ 54
☿ 5 ♉ 56
♀ 1 ♓ 40
♂ 20 ♒ 20
♃ 3 ♋ 34
♄ 24 ♉ 45
♅ 9 ♉ 34
♆ 14 ♉ 33
♇ 17 ♏ 10 ℞

9 MONDAY

10 TUESDAY

3:18 ○ 20 ♎ 0
Moon Void of Course:
from 12:59 to 23:18 ♏

11 WEDNESDAY

12 THURSDAY

13 FRIDAY

Moon Void of Course:
from 1:34 to 11:48 ♐

14 SATURDAY

By Mars contrary to the Monarchy
Of the great fisherman
will be in trouble
The young red king will take over
the government.
The traitors will act on a misty day.

TAURUS
April 20th – May 20th
Fixed – Earth
Negative – Personal
Rules the 2nd House
Ruled by Venus

15 SUNDAY

Moon Void of Course:
from 16:24 to 24:00

☉	24 ♈	46
☿	14 ♉	5
♀	9 ♓	1
♂	25 ♒	34
♃	4 ♋	29
♄	25 ♉	1
♅	9 ♑	35 ℞
♆	14 ♑	35
♇	17 ♏	0 ℞

16 MONDAY

Moon Void of Course:
from 0:00 to 0:15 ♑

17 TUESDAY

18 WEDNESDAY

7:03 ◑ 27 ♉ 59

Moon Void of Course:
from 7:03 to 10:53 ♒

19 THURSDAY

20 FRIDAY

Moon Void of Course:
from 17:42 to 17:57 ♓

21 SATURDAY

A mass of men approach from
Slavonia,
The Destroyer (Neapolluon), will ruin
the old city:
He will see his Roman Empire quite
desolated,
Then he would not know how to
extinguish the great flame.

In other words, through the use of potions and natural cures Nostradamus made his mind silent in order to tap other more sensitive and subtle areas of his consciousness.

He also employed rituals and other magical methods and incantations which were intended to put him in a trance state so that he could, in his owns words "become available to God's will."

If we consider that God's will in this context, may be simply that subtle "self" that exists beneath the areas of conscious awareness, at a level connected with the cosmic consciousness, then perhaps Nostradamus' gift was simply an ability to get in touch with the universe at a level that the rest of mankind does not achieve. Perhaps somewhere in the far reaches of existence there is an avenue down which we can all go to see the future and all it will contain.

It is not as though Nostradamus has been the only one to find methods of tapping the future. There have been a significant number of other prophets able to achieve the same results and even in many cases make similar predictions.

There is a further aspect to this strange and complex notion of time travel: that as well as past prophets having a lot say about their future, with much of what they said influencing perhaps the way that it unfolds, there is also the fascinating concept of those about whom the prophets made predictions being concerned with the predictions themselves.

Ready to flight he will desert,
The chief adversary will be victorious.
The rear guard will make a defense,
Those who falter dying in the
white country.

TAURUS
Moon in exaltation
Jupiter strong
Pluto in detriment
Uranus in fall

---

22 SUNDAY

Moon Void of Course:
from 13:04 to 20:58 ♈

☉	1	♉ 37
☿	17	♉ 27
♀	16	♓ 34
♂	0	♓ 48
♃	5	♋ 30
♄	25	♉ 12
♅	9	♉ 34 ℞
♆	14	♉ 34 ℞
♇	16	♏ 49 ℞

---

23 MONDAY

---

24 TUESDAY

Moon Void of Course:
from 13:33 to 21:03 ♉

25 WEDNESDAY

4:27 ● 4 ♀ 43

26 THURSDAY

Moon Void of Course:
from 12:45 to 20:12 ♓

27 FRIDAY

28 SATURDAY

Moon Void of Course:
from 10:08 to 20:39 ♋

*The great Empire will soon be
exchanged for a little place...
A small petty place of tiny area,
In the middle of which
He will come to lay down his sceptre.*

TAURUS
Stone: Emerald
Metal: Copper
Color: Green

29 SUNDAY

☉	8	♉	26
☿	16	♉	7 ℞
♀	24	♓	15
♂	6	♓	2
♃	6	♋	37
♄	25	♑	19
♅	9	♑	30 ℞
♆	14	♑	32 ℞
♇	16	♏	38 ℞

30 MONDAY

Moon Void of Course:
from 17:21 to 24:00

Napoleon retreats from Russia.

Imagine that you, the reader, were to find a prediction about yourself within "The Centuries" written by Nostradamus. That one day you were reading one of the prophet's books and you recognized your own name therein!

That on the following pages of the book there were, laid out before you, the events that you could expect to unfold in your own life and the effect these events would have on the world of your own time.

You would, perhaps feel a little like a robot without the power to direct your own life. If each event that you undertook had been viewed already by someone living long before you, the effect would undoubtedly be disturbing in the least.

And yet, if we take a close look at the prophecies of the master prophet, this must have been the case for more than one individual since Nostradamus died in the 16th century.

And such an experience is supposed to have happened to none other than Adolph Hitler, as we will see in the next month of May.

MAY

The sun, twenty degrees into Taurus
(May 10th),
There will be a tremendous earthquake,
The great theater filled (with people)
will be ruined,
The air, heaven and the Earth
will be dark and obscure
When the unbelievers call on God
and the saints.

TAURUS
Animal: Bull
Bird: Swan
Fish: Mallet
Plant: Sycamore

What seeds Aries has planted, the hard working Taurus will grow. Strong, calm and silent, you have an ability to nurture and grow anything in the farm, in the garden, in the house or in the stock-broker's office.

Being gifted with a beautiful voice, you love art, play a musical instrument and are often found among great performers. Handsome and with a sensitivity to beauty, this sign, ruled by Venus, can be lazy and indulgent in the good things of life such as food, luxurious toilet goods, sex and a comfortable house.

Before you find your soul mate, your passive and sensual Taurus nature will make you think it over many times; you won't make any promises until you are sure you have the right choice. Strongly attracted to the opposite sex you will make people attracted to you rather than chasing them around. When you have finally decided on a partner, your steady, protective, nurturing personality becomes extremely possessive.

You usually own a house and love spending time in it and devoting yourself to your family. You like to collect things and usually two or three of each item can be found collected in your house.

You are stubborn, rigid and hate any kind of change. You will not let anyone push you around, but are easily seduced into things. You are slow at making any kind of decision and won't step on anyone's feet to get your way. Rather you will move aside and wait until the right moment has come. But when your patience is abused you will experience the angry side of your nature: once the bull is irritated, he charges in full force. You don't easily get angry but when you do, the ones who angered you will remember.

Earthy and practical you are a builder and can do almost anything with your hands. When you combine your dexterity with the Venusian touch, what you do looks good if not remarkable.

The Taurus has bought the land and built his home, now the soul needs to discover the realms of the mind. Fixed to his post, the Taurus goes towards Gemini he has the task of welcoming changes, natural to his following Sun sign.

CENTURY OF THE SUN

Gallipoli – World War I – heralded as one of man's greatest battles – Nostradamus at least might have understood this. But on such a scale there could have been no comparison with the slaughter in battles of his age.

The romantics of war, those that wish us to believe in the sanctity of slaughter for the sake of their territorial restrictions, call this man "an unknown warrior!"

ADOLF HITLER AS A BABY

Born in Linz Austria, on the shores of the Danube, this child of poor customs officials was destined to seduce the entire German nation into an orgy of nazism through eloquent lies and half-truths. Imperial Japan would join his Axis Alliance during World War II.

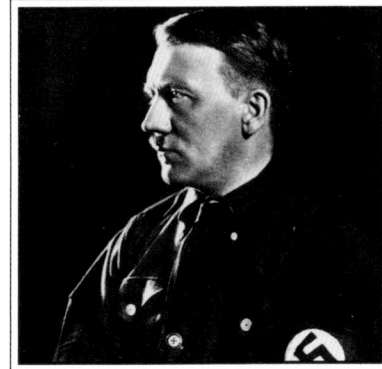

HITLER

THE 20TH CENTURY would be a shock for any prophet! "Few will be found who wish to stay in their places," wrote Nostradamus and this is, to say the least, an understatement.

Very little of what would have been the environment of the 16th century remains today.

In this last set of one hundred years we have gone from the steam engine to space flight with flying machines planned to be developed that will fly at more than 24 times the speed of sound. We have experienced more deaths from war than almost the whole of the previous thousand years put together and exhibited a greater capacity for slaughter than even Nostradamus could have naturally conceived of.

And yet he did. For Nostradamus saw Hitler himself, the single man in this century, perhaps, who caused more suffering and havoc than any human being in the whole history of mankind.

And not only did Nostradamus see Hitler, but if the stories are true, Hitler saw Nostradamus see him.

The story of Hitler's awareness of Nostradamus' predictions came to light in its true form when the book *Nostradamus and the Millennium* was being compiled.

The story goes that Frau Goebbels, the wife of Hitler's notorious propaganda minister, was sitting in bed reading a copy of a book which contained extracts from "The Centuries," Nostradamus' record of his predictions. Suddenly she sat up and exclaimed

to her husband that what she was reading was about none other than the great Fuehrer himself and what she was reading had been written almost four hundred years before! Evidently Goebells was asleep to her gesticulations of astonishment but with further efforts and reading out loud she managed to rouse him from slumber and explain what it was all about.

Goebells, with his nose for publicity, quickly realized the potential of the predictions and immediately went to work to hire an astrologer. The first reports of the interpretation of Nostradamus' predictions regarding Hitler may not have been so positive as Goebells wanted so that, so the story goes, the hired astrologer had to slightly alter the predictions in

Hitler and Mussolini used the tragedy of the Spanish Civil War as a testing ground to sharpen weapons and strategies later to be used for world conquest. Nazi and Italian armaments helped kill six hundred thousand people between 1936 and 1939.

HITLER AND FRANCO

MUSSOLINI

order to make a satisfactory interpretation which could be used as propaganda against the English – "How Hitler's Germany wins the war" and such like statements.

Fliers were printed with the Nostradamus propaganda on them and dropped over England by airplanes in hundreds of thousands – hopefully to sour the English confidence by demonstrating the predictions of the famous prophet against them.

Churchill is then said to have replied with the correct information that Nostradamus had actually said that Hitler's effort would fail. These flyers were then dropped over Germany – a sort of 'airmail" service special!

The story intrigued the author and editors and the publishers of *Nostradamus and the Millennium*

to such an extent that they dispatched a researcher to the London War Museum to look for pictures and check out the story. Here, an expert on matters of the Second World War spying and propaganda machines both in Germany and England declared that the story was true in every respect except one – the most important one. The whole effort of forging Nostradamus quatrains and sending the flyers over England and Germany actually happened, but it was not operated by Goebells at all, but by Churchill's British Black Intelligence Group in England.

They made up the story about Goebells' wife reading Nostradamus, printed the flyers and dropped them over England with false information on them and

then printed and distributed the English answer as well!

It is generally held to be true, however, that Hitler was aware of Nostradamus' predictions about him but he did not pursue the potential use of them, perhaps because they weren't exactly complimentary.

This story does, however, open the door to further inquiry about our future and the people and events that Nostradamus gave us a preview of.

Which of the coming names that are so often contained within his quatrains might already apply to living characters in future history? And how many of these characters are going to spot their existence in the future of the past? And in the event that they do, how would this recognition and the

The stock market crash – past... and future?

1

TUESDAY

20:18 ◐ 11 ♌ 11

Moon Void of Course:
from 0:00 to 0:08 ♌

2

WEDNESDAY

Moon Void of Course:
from 6:06 to 24:00

3

THURSDAY

Moon Void of Course:
from 0:00 to 7:18 ♏

4

FRIDAY

5

SATURDAY

Moon Void of Course:
from 8:17 to 17:28 ♎

*The imitations of gold and silver
will become inflated
which after the rape are thrown
into the fire,
After discovering all is exhausted
and dissipated by the debt.
All scripts and bonds are wiped out.*

TAURUS
Rules the neck and the throat
Identity: The Builder
Keyword: Stability
Keynote: I have

6 SUNDAY

☉	15	♉	13
☿	12	♉	0 ℞
♀	2	♈	4
♂	11	♓	16
♃	7	♋	48
♄	25	♉	20 ℞
♅	9	♉	23 ℞
♆	14	♉	29 ℞
♇	16	♏	26 ℞

7 MONDAY

Moon Void of Course:
from 19:59 to 24:00

8 TUESDAY

Moon Void of Course:
from 0:00 to 5:22 ♏

9

WEDNESDAY

19:31 ○ 18 ♏ 54

10

THURSDAY

Moon Void of Course:
from 8:28 to 17:56 ♐

11

FRIDAY

12

SATURDAY

Moon Void of Course:
from 1:48 to 24:00

*From the deepest part
of Western Europe
A young child will be born
to poor people:
Who by his speech will seduce
a great multitude,
His reputation will increase in
the Kingdom of the East.*

TAURUS
Cashiers, financial agents,
masseurs, doctors,
mechanics, foreman,
agriculture, farmers,
chefs and cooks.

13 SUNDAY

Moon Void of Course:
from 0:00 to 6:21 ♉

☉ 21 ♉ 59
☿ 8 ♉ 33 ℞
♀ 9 ♈ 58
♂ 16 ♓ 29
♃ 9 ♋ 4
♄ 25 ♉ 17 ℞
♅ 9 ♉ 15 ℞
♆ 14 ♉ 24 ℞
♇ 16 ♏ 14 ℞

14 MONDAY

15 TUESDAY

Moon Void of Course:
from 8:17 to 17:30 ♒

16 WEDNESDAY

17 THURSDAY

19:45 ◑ 26 ♎ 38
Moon Void of Course:
from 19:45 to 24:00

18 FRIDAY

Moon Void of Course:
from 0:00 to 1:54 ♓

19 SATURDAY

Original painting by J. Frankl, after being interred in the Auschwitz concentration camp during World War II.

"Es qualmte in dicken
Schwaden, und da die
Verbrennung der
Gemordeten bei nur
ungenügender
Temperatur
durchgeführt wurde,
roch es in der ganzen
Umgebung nach
verbrannten Fleisch".

possible knowledge of their own future, affect their lives to come?

Continuing our investigation of how successful Nostradamus' predictions have been, we might just look at the one concerned with "paper money."

"*The imitations of gold and silver will become inflated*
Which after the rape are thrown into the fire,
After discovering all is exhausted and dissipated by the debt.
All scripts and bonds are wiped out."

One of the most dramatic parts of this prediction is the mention of what amounts to paper money. In the 16th century the concept of money as debt was very young and took the form of silver merchant's receipts for deposited gold, silver or valuables. These receipts were then usable as exchange but in no way did they represent the paper money that we are accustomed to today and Nostradamus' vision of a time when currency and inflation would be the norm is truly spectacular.

The whole philosophy of money was nowhere near the development of being a global energy as it is now and yet he was able to look forward and see the day when not only global finance was common but also in disarray.

The above quatrain was taken to indicate the stock market crash of the year 1929, perhaps the most dramatic in history, but is seen also as an indication of this century's financial problems in America.

In the original text, *Nostradamus and the Millennium* the prediction was made that other stock market collapses would be the aim of this prediction and of course we have seen two more since then in New York and Hong Kong so that this particular prediction might be said to have been highly successful!

The statement that gold and silver "will become inflated" also, of course, applies to the general printing of money against gold reserves. In the 1930s originally, the British Bank of England decided that it was no longer necessary to

have only as much currency in circulation as there was gold value on reserve and started printing money at the rate of three times that of the gold reserve value.

This alone can be seen as a direct fulfillment of the predictions.

How many more financial crashes do we have to face in our future which could perhaps have been avoided if Nostradamus' words of warning were heeded more closely.

Of course it would be naive to suggest that the complex and multi-dimensional business of financial operation would benefit directly from specific observations made over four centuries ago. Nostradamus was no money expert but the overall pictures he created for our understanding do contain great areas of wisdom which relate to a larger field than that of money or government. They present a world wide painting of life and must be considered as a whole area of predication rather than a particular and focused method of prophecy.

111111111

*...Human flesh through death is
burned to ashes...*

GEMINI
May 21st – June 20th
Mutable – Air
Positive – Personal
Rules the 3rd House
Ruled by Mercury

20 SUNDAY

Moon Void of Course:
from 4:42 to 6:31 ♈

☉ 28 ♉ 44
☿ 8 ♉ 15
♀ 17 ♈ 58
♂ 21 ♓ 40
♃ 10 ♋ 24
♄ 25 ♉ 9 ℞
♅ 9 ♉ 4 ℞
♆ 14 ♑ 17 ℞
♇ 16 ♏ 3 ℞

21 MONDAY

Moon Void of Course:
from 23:52 to 24:00

22 TUESDAY

Moon Void of Course:
from 0:00 to 7:42 ♉

23

WEDNESDAY

Moon Void of Course:
from 23:14 to 24:00

24

THURSDAY

11:47 ● 3 ♓ 3

Moon Void of Course:
from 0:00 to 7:00 ♓

25

FRIDAY

26

SATURDAY

Moon Void of Course:
from 0:18 to 6:34 ♋

Near the harbors within two cities,
There will happen two scourges the
like of which was never before seen,
Famine, pestilence within,
people put out by the sword.
They cry for help
from the great immortal God!

GEMINI
North node in exaltation
Saturn strong
Jupiter in detriment
South node in fall

27 SUNDAY

☉	5 ♓ 28
☿	11 ♉ 33
♀	26 ♈ 2
♂	26 ♓ 51
♃	11 ♋ 48
♄	24 ♑ 57 ℞
♅	8 ♑ 52 ℞
♆	14 ♑ 10 ℞
♇	15 ♏ 51 ℞

28 MONDAY

Moon Void of Course:
from 4:34 to 8:29 ♌

29 TUESDAY

Moon Void of Course:
from 12:13 to 24:00

30

WEDNESDAY

Moon Void of Course:
from 0:00 to 14:08 ♍

31

THURSDAY

8:11 ☽ 9 ♍ 38

JUNE

He will come to take himself to
the corner of Luna (the moon)
Where he will be taken and placed
on alien land...

GEMINI
Stone: Agate
Metal: Mercury
Color: Bright blue

Sociable, charming and liked by everyone, your head is always full of clever remarks, puns and stories. Ruled by Mercury, you love intellectual pursuits and live mostly in your mind. Communication is your ball game and you love to read books and talk to friends. Your great ability for expression will make you an eloquent public speaker, humorist, radio or TV employee, journalist, teacher and actor. Although you like to learn and know a lot of things, you hate tedious study and prefer to borrow your knowledge from others. The Gemini knows a little about a lot of things.

Mutable by nature your dual personality reflects any change in your environment. Happy, charming and wonderful at times you can magically become pessimistic and depressed. Quick and versatile, you can accomplish many things at the same time. Always in search of variety and movement, you find it hard to stay in the same place or do the same thing for very long. Restless and nervous you love travel and any change in situations. Being a Gemini you can go through many different pro-

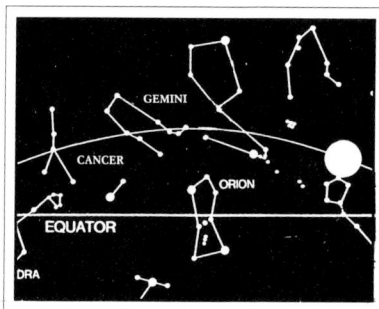

fessions in one life-time and be extremely capable in each one, but your lack of single-mindedness prevents you from extracting the maximum out of any career.

In romance you are unpredictable, always changing your mind and unable to settle down. One side of you falls in love and the other denies that feeling. You are a natural bachelor and prefer flirting with whoever fits with you mood of the moment. If you enter a long-term relationship, it will be with someone in perfect menta harmony with you, someone who can cope with your mood fluctuations.

Your quick mind makes an excellent telephone operator journalist, reporter, as well as stock broker or dealer. In fact you car excel in any career which has variety and where you can use your intelligence.

As the soul goes through the intellectual path of communication, it remains on the surface never touching the emotiona depths. This is what the Gemini goes into as it goes towards Cancer he needs to dive into his emotions and learn about the nurturing nature of his following Sun sign.

GLOBAL VILLAGE

*Pestilences extinguished, the world
becomes small
For a long time the lands will be
inhabited in peace.
People will travel safely by air,
(over) land, seas and wave.
Then wars will start again.*

THE QUATRAIN OPPOSITE this page is commonly believed by most Nostradamus interpreters, to apply to the period following World War II. It is a strangely compelling verse as it looks, with extraordinary clarity and brevity, both on the bright side and the dark side about a time which is our own.

We are in the time of the "Global Village," a time that has enormous potential for good and bad news and here, Nostradamus' news of the future says it all.

"Pestilences extinguished, the world becomes small..." The Pestilence to Nostradamus was the plague that he had so much to do with in his own time. And his reference to the small world refers to the advent of rapid communication and transport networks which have so much reduced our planet and made it so easy for us to have access anywhere in so short a time.

And, according to the second line, we have a long time of peace after the Second World War in which we will be able to take advantage of the assets of that rapid and "safe" transport across the globe.

But the peace is not for ever – "Then wars will start again," – a dire prediction of our future potential. Sadly he is not specific about when or what form these wars will take – and even if he had been, it is doubtful that those in a position to do anything about it would pay any attention.

But then there is also the thought that war has been going on almost continuously in one part of the world or another since shortly after the Second World War, so perhaps his prediction of peace is at fault instead.

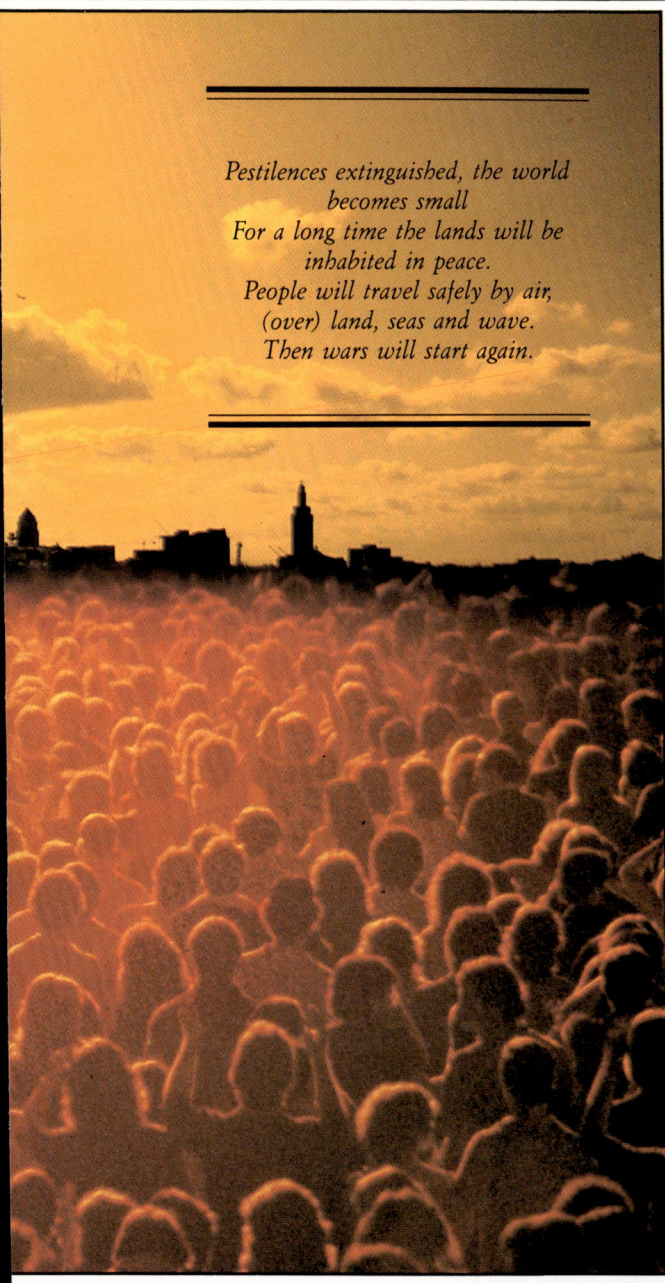

John Fitzgerald Kennedy and his wife Jacqueline seemed like the perfect couple at top of the US political tree. Whatever they we was not to last in face of the anxiou American criminal world.

The great man will be struck down
in the day by a thunderbolt,
The evil deed predicted by the bearer
of a petition:
According to the prediction another
falls at night time.
Conflict in Reins, London,
and pestilence in Tuscany.

GEMINI
Animal: Monkey
Bird: Cockatoo
Fish: Chub
Plant: Ash

1

FRIDAY

Moon Void of Course:
from 13:13 to 23:31 ♎

2

SATURDAY

The sudden death of the first personage
Will have caused a change and put
another to rule:
Soon but too late he comes to high
position, of young age,
By land and sea it will be necessary
to fear him.

GEMINI
Rules shoulders and arms
Identity: The Communicator
Keyword: Diversity
Keynote: I think

3 SUNDAY

☉	12 ♓	11
☿	17 ♉	57
♀	4 ♉	9
♂	1 ♈	59
♃	13 ♋	14
♄	24 ♉	41 ℞
♅	8 ♉	38 ℞
♆	14 ♉	1 ℞
♇	15 ♏	41 ℞

4 MONDAY

Moon Void of Course:
from 0:33 to 11:22 ♏

5 TUESDAY

6
WEDNESDAY

Moon Void of Course:
from 12:54 to 23:59 ♐

7
THURSDAY

8
FRIDAY

11:01 ○ 17 ♐ 24

Moon Void of Course:
from 11:01 to 24:00

9
SATURDAY

Moon Void of Course:
from 0:00 to 12:12 ♑

Before the people, blood will be spilt,
It will not come far from
the high heavens:
But for a long time it will not
be heard,
The spirit of a single man will bear
witness to it.

GEMINI
Post and telephone workers,
writers, poets,
reporters, journalists,
dealers, book-keepers,
advertising agents,
radio and public speakers.

10 SUNDAY

⊙	18 ♓	52
☿	26 ♉	57
♀	12 ♉	19
♂	7 ♈	4
♃	14 ♋	42
♄	24 ♉	20 ℞
♅	8 ♉	23 ℞
♆	13 ♉	51 ℞
♇	15 ♏	31

11 MONDAY

Moon Void of Course:
from 22:58 to 23:09 ♒

12 TUESDAY

13
WEDNESDAY

Moon Void of Course:
from 17:57 to 24:00

14
THURSDAY

Moon Void of Course:
from 0:00 to 8:00 ♓

15
FRIDAY

16
SATURDAY

4:48 ◑ 24 ♓ 48
Moon Void of Course:
from 4:48 to 13:55 ♈

Nine will be set apart
from the human flock
separated from judgement and
counsel:
Their fate to be determined
on departure...
...The unripe fruit will be the source
of great scandal
Great blame, to the other great praise.

Far distant from his realm,
sent on a dangerous journey
He will lead a great army
and keep it for himself,
The King will hold his nation hostage
He will plunder the whole country
on his return.

CANCER
June 21st – July 21st
Cardinal – Water
Negative – Personal
Rules the 4th House
Ruled by the Moon

17 SUNDAY

☉	25 ♓	34
☿	8 ♓	19
♀	20 ♉	33
♂	12 ♈	7
♃	16 ♋	13
♄	23 ♉	57 ℞
♅	8 ♉	6 ℞
♆	13 ♉	41 ℞
♇	15 ♏	22 ℞

18 MONDAY

Moon Void of Course:
from 11:44 to 16:43 ☿

19 TUESDAY

20

WEDNESDAY

Moon Void of Course:
from 8:26 to 17:15 ♓

21

THURSDAY

Moon Void of Course:
from 21:13 to 24:00

22

FRIDAY

18:55 ● 1 ♋ 5

Moon Void of Course:
from 0:00 to 17:09 ♋

23

SATURDAY

The speeches of Lake Leman (Geneva)
become angered.
The days drag out into weeks,
Then months, then years,
then all will fail,
The authorities will damn
their useless powers.

CANCER
Jupiter in exaltation
Mercury strong
Saturn in detriment
Mars in fall

24 SUNDAY

Moon Void of Course:
from 17:53 to 18:25 ♌

☉ 2 ♋ 15
☿ 21 ♓ 50
♀ 28 ♈ 48
♂ 17 ♈ 6
♃ 17 ♋ 45
♄ 23 ♉ 30 ℞
♅ 7 ♉ 50 ℞
♆ 13 ♉ 30 ℞
♇ 15 ♏ 15 ℞

25 MONDAY

26 TUESDAY

Moon Void of Course:
from 18:28 to 22:42 ♍

27 WEDNESDAY

28 THURSDAY

Moon Void of Course:
from 17:42 to 24:00

29 FRIDAY

22:07 ◑ 7 ♎ 54

Moon Void of Course:
from 0:00 to 6:47 ♎

30 SATURDAY

JULY

In the year 1999 and seven months
The great King of Terror will come
from the sky
He will resurrect Ghengis Khan
Before and after war rules happily.

CANCER
Stone: Pearl
Metal: Silver
Color: Silver

Moody, imaginative and sensitive the Cancerian can go from laughing heartily to a cranky mood. Deeply insecure, you find comfort and happiness in your warm and comfortable home, your family and friends. As much as you need love, comfort and protection, you love to nurture and be needed by your beloved ones.

Being of the element Water, you are deeply emotional. Like the crab, you are extremely tenacious, but a cruel word or a harsh voice and you retreat in solitude. But disappearing from the world is going away from what you need the most in that moment: the warm support and caring of your friends.

You love things of the past: history, old paintings, antiquities and old memories. You can recall anything said or heard years ago in every minute detail. Once in a while you may get the blues and think of all the wonderful things you used to do.

Ruled by the Moon you have a tendency to absorb the world around you, so be careful which friends you choose and which environment you live in. You love pets, children and anything that grows. Attracted by the mystical

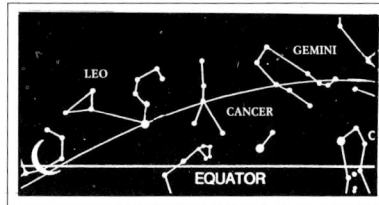

and occult you feel and sense things directly. You are creative and especially skilled in acting, composing and design. Your love for the sea can make you an excellent sailor while your affinity with liquids will make you a good barman. Your homey nature will lead you into housekeeping, hotel-keeping and cooking.

You know the value of money and are very economical, sometimes to the extreme. Money represents security for many of the Cancerians, but the bank account won't give the vulnerable crab the protection he longs for, no matter how substantial it is.

In the affairs of the heart it will take a long time to really know you. Sensitive and loyal, you value security as much as your partner. A natural parent with a strong nurturing nature, your children will have all the love they need.

In Cancer the soul enters the emotions for the first time. It has traveled deep into the unconscious, but has left a deep insecurity behind. As the homey nature of the Cancer goes towards Leo, it needs to acquire the inner strength of his following Sun sign.

THE LAST DAYS OF THE ROCK

Paul VI's strict conservative piety.

John XXIII's generous figure and compassionate image contrasts sharply with...

PERHAPS THE MOST POWER-FUL AREA of our lives today, that Nostradamus was fascinated by, is religion. In some respects the powers that be in our religious world today, haven't greatly altered their approach to life in the intervening four hundred years. Organized religion is just as prejudiced and fixed today as it was in the 16th century of France, where the Spanish Inquisition chased Nostradamus all over Europe for part of his life in an attempt to stop his predictions.

THE LAS
"RUIN APPROACHES, NOT OF YOUR WALL

NOSTRADAMUS

O vast Rome, your ruin is approaching
Not that of your walls
but of your lifeblood and substance.
Wickedness will work such
a horrible attack through writings
that all will be persecuted.

C10 Q65

In 1555 Nostradamus first published his predictions outlining the fates of the last six popes. His quatrains closely resemble the vision of Malachi, who lived four centuries before. He even describes John Paul I as the moon (Malachi "De medietate lunae") and John Paul II as "The Work of the Sun" (Malachi "De labore solis"). Malachi's original manuscript was not discovered in the Vatican Archives until 1590 – 24 years after the death of Nostradamus.

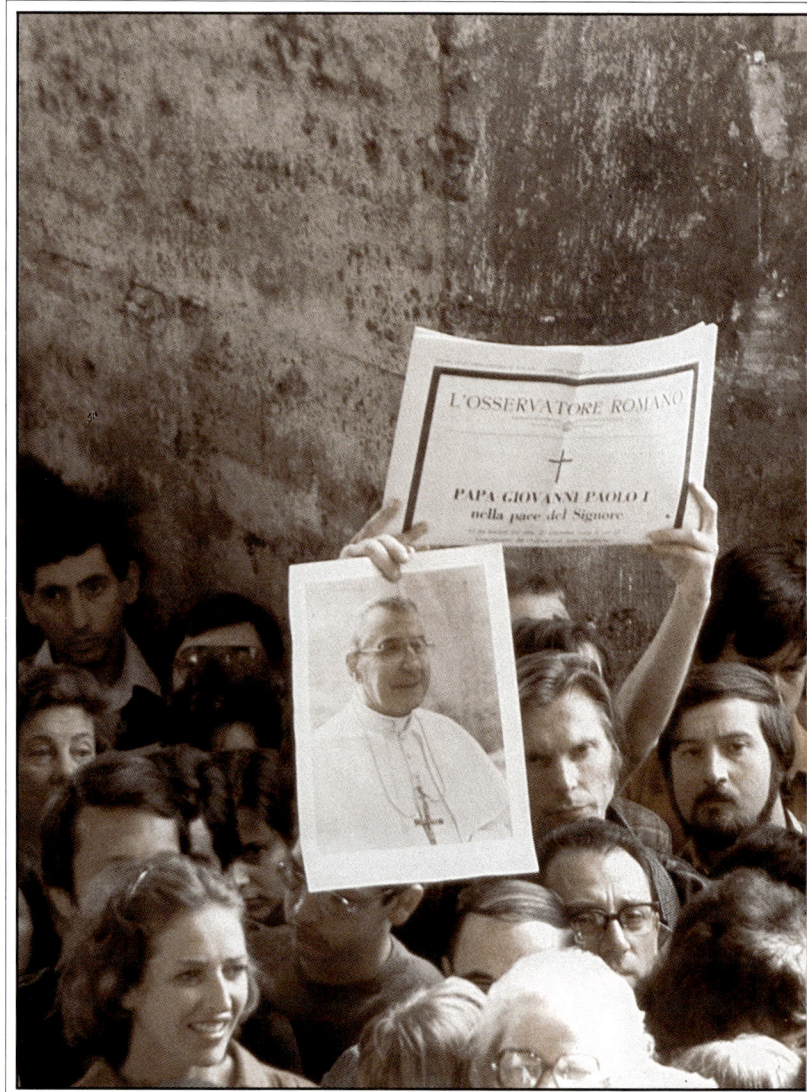

ONTIFFS –
JT OF YOUR LIFEBLOOD AND SUBSTANCE"

MALACHI

IN PERSECUTIONE EXTREMA SACRAE ROMANAE ECCLESIAE, SEDEBIT PETRUS ROMANUS QUI PASCET OVES IN MULTIS TRIBULATIONIBUS: QUIBUS TRANSACTIS, CIVITAS SPTICOLLIS DIRUETUR, ET JUDEX TREMENDUS JUDICABIT POPULUMSUUM. AMEN.

IN THE FINAL PERSECUTION OF THE HOLY ROMAN CHURCH, PETER THE ROMAN WILL OCCUPY THE SEE, WHO WILL GUIDE HIS FLOCK THROUGH NUMEROUS TRIBULA-TIONS. THESE TRIBULATIONS PAST, THE TOWN OF SEVEN HILLS WILL BE DESTROYED AND THE TERRIBLE JUDGE SHALL JUDGE THE PEOPLE.

In 1138, Malachi, an Irish priest, visited Rome. In an ecstatic trance he had a vision of the entire succession of 112 popes. His precise descriptions of each pontiff have proved to be uncannily accurate, even to the giving of actual names. In 1986 there are only two popes left in the succession before the final fall of the Church of Rome.

*For four years, the Seat will be held
for some little good.
One will accede to it
who is more worldly.
Ravenna and Pisa,
Verona will support him,
desirous of elevating the Papal cross.*

CANCER
Animal: Crab and cat
Bird: Owl
Fish: Catfish
Plant: Willow

1 SUNDAY

Moon Void of Course:
from 4:01 to 18:01 ♏

☉ 8 ♋ 55
☿ 6 ♋ 49
♀ 7 ♓ 6
♂ 22 ♈ 2
♃ 19 ♋ 18
♄ 23 ♉ 1 ℞
♅ 7 ♉ 33 ℞
♆ 13 ♉ 19 ℞
♇ 15 ♏ 8 ℞

2 MONDAY

3 TUESDAY

Moon Void of Course:
from 16:06 to 24:00

4 WEDNESDAY

Moon Void of Course:
from 0:00 to 6:35 ♐

5 THURSDAY

6 FRIDAY

Moon Void of Course:
from 10:18 to 18:39 ♑

7 SATURDAY

After the very aged Pope's death
Will be elected a Roman of good age:
He will be accused of weakening
the Holy See and will last a long time,
doing controversial work.

CANCER
Rules the breasts and stomach
Identity: The Nurturer
Keyword: Sympathy
Keynote: I feel

8 SUNDAY

1:23 ○ 15 ♑ 39

⊙ 15 ♋ 36
☿ 21 ♋ 52
♀ 15 ♓ 26
♂ 26 ♈ 52
♃ 20 ♋ 52
♄ 22 ♑ 31 ℞
♅ 7 ♑ 16 ℞
♆ 13 ♑ 8 ℞
♇ 15 ♏ 3 ℞

9 MONDAY

Moon Void of Course:
from 0:25 to 5:07 ♒

10 TUESDAY

11 WEDNESDAY

Moon Void of Course:
from 12:06 to 13:29 ♓

12 THURSDAY

13 FRIDAY

Moon Void of Course:
from 5:38 to 19:36 ♈

14 SATURDAY

The one elected Pope
will be mocked by his electors,
this enterprising and prudent person
will suddenly be reduced to silence.
They cause him to die because of his
too great goodness and mildness.
Stricken by fear, they will lead him
to his death in the night.

CANCER
Sailor, naval captains,
housekeeper, mid-wife,
laundress, barman,
builders, merchants and
real-estate agents.

15 SUNDAY

11:04 ◑ 22 ♈ 43

Moon Void of Course:
from 14:09 to 23:29 ☿

⊙ 22 ♋ 16
☿ 5 ♌ 50
♀ 23 ♓ 49
♂ 1 ♉ 36
♃ 22 ♋ 26
♄ 22 ♑ 0 ℞
♅ 6 ♑ 59 ℞
♆ 12 ♑ 56 ℞
♇ 15 ♏ 0 ℞

16 MONDAY

17 TUESDAY

Moon Void of Course:
from 17:02 to 24:00

18 **WEDNESDAY**

Moon Void of Course:
from 0:00 to 1:32 ♓

19 **THURSDAY**

20 **FRIDAY**

Moon Void of Course:
from 2:38 to 2:44 ♋

21 **SATURDAY**

In the brief 30 days of his life as pontiff, John Paul I endeared himself to the people by his sunny, very human charisma and a natural sense of compassionate honesty. A born reformist, he immediately enraged the conservatives in the Curia and threatened those who had secretly abused the privileges of power in the previous years.

In this month of 1990 we will look a little then at those words he uttered about our present day religions, most specifically about the Roman Catholic Church.

Nostradamus was quite accustomed to dealing with large issues – the collapse of a nation, the fall of a Royal House and even the eventual curtailment of a world religion – one of the greatest forces behind man's evolution.

The prophet, therefore, gave not the slightest tremor when writing about what he saw as the collapse of the great Catholic Church during the very last years of the 20th century – our century.

His message was powerful and poetic and concerned with the Popes who would fill the last frames of the Vatican walls before the last Papal seat was filled by a St Peter who would bring the mighty Catholic Church full circle – "Alpha to Omega" – a cycle is complete.

Before the very last date book of this century is published we will know whether or not this prediction has been fulfilled. If it is, no doubt, there will be much unrest and chaos to ensue and in many ways it would, of course, be preferable that no such event occurs. On the other hand, life is change and the present state of the Catholic Church leaves much to be desired.

The main thrust of Nostradamus' quatrains on the final days of the Church take the form of a very dramatic statement that the last Pope, St Peter, will be dragged through the streets of the Vatican and murdered by his own people. The Pope before last will be named Clement and for months before the end of the Catholic reign there will be a schism within the Vatican which will eventually result in the collapse of the official Church.

There are other stories that have come from previous predictions, not by Nostradamus, which talk of the eventual discovery of the body of Jesus Christ within the vaults of the Vatican. Such a discovery would, of course, completely deflate the whole basis of the Catholic Church to the extent that Catholic dogma stands upon the foundations of the resurrection of Jesus Christ after the time on the cross. This is, however, only a story!

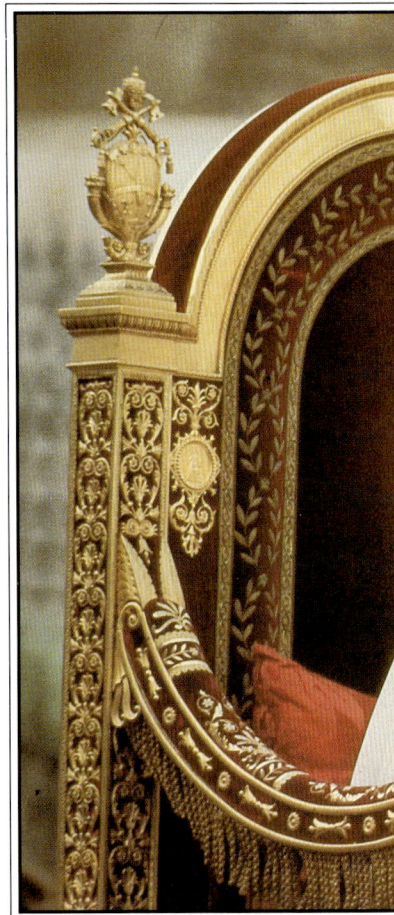

As always in Nostradamus' predictions, it is impossible to say whether or not the chosen quatrains actually refer to the events we believe they might. There are literally hundreds and hundreds of

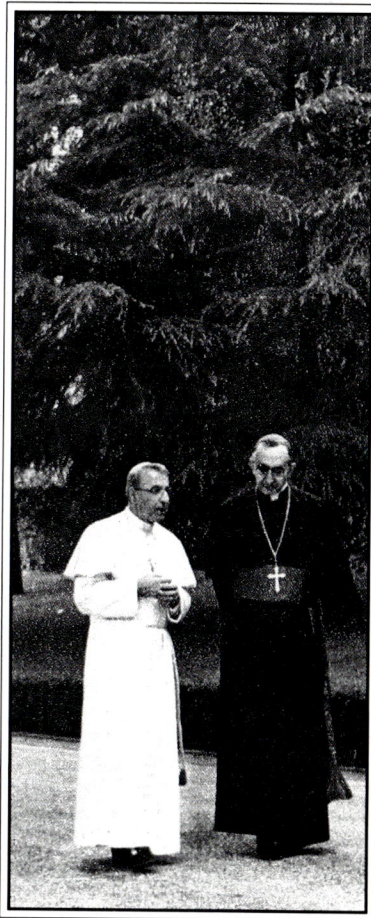

quatrains and of course, in our history there are many thousands of
events to which they could potentially be applied.

It is hard to deny that many of
the quatrains have been accurately
married up with events but to see
them as being referenced to future
events, as yet unfolded, is hard to
do and those referring to the Cath-

olic Church at the end of this century could easily be totally off tar-
get.

Nevertheless, there are certain pointers for those familiar
with the Prophet's work and many
of them do appear within the
quatrains that appear to be concerned with the Popes. Watch this
space!

Walking with his secretary of state Cardinal
Villot. On the night before his death, John
Paul had given a list to the Cardinal: a
complete reshuffle of staff within the power
structure of the Vatican. Villot later issued
false statements to the police and the press
about the circumstances surrounding the
death of the pope. The controversial list has
never been found.

A short while before the Holy
Monarch (John Paul II) is murdered
Castor and Pollux (Twin named Pope,
John Paul II)
In the papacy, a bearded star
(Halley's Comet)
Public treasure is emptied...

LEO
July 22nd – August 21st
Fixed – Fire
Positive – Interpersonal
Rules the 5th House
Ruled by the Sun

22 SUNDAY

2:54 ● 29 ♋ 4
2:38 Total solar eclipse

Moon Void of Course:
from 2:54 to 4:29 ♌

☉ 28 ♋ 57
☿ 18 ♌ 20
♀ 2 ♋ 13
♂ 6 ♈ 15
♃ 24 ♋ 0
♄ 21 ♑ 29 ℞
♅ 6 ♑ 43 ℞
♆ 12 ♑ 45 ℞
♇ 14 ♏ 58 ℞

23 MONDAY

Moon Void of Course:
from 16:40 to 24:00

24 TUESDAY

Moon Void of Course:
from 0:00 to 8:17 ♍

25 WEDNESDAY

26 THURSDAY

Moon Void of Course:
from 5:49 to 15:19 ♎

27 FRIDAY

28 SATURDAY

Very near the Tiber death threatens,
Shortly after the great flood.
The head of the church
will be taken prisoner and cast out,
the castle (St. Angelo)
and the Palace (Vatican) in flames.

LEO
Pluto in exaltation
Mars strong
Uranus in detriment
Neptune in fall

☉	5 ♌	38
☿	29 ♌	19
♀	10 ♋	40
♂	10 ♈	46
♃	25 ♋	34
♄	20 ♑	59 ℞
♅	6 ♑	29 ℞
♆	12 ♑	35 ℞
♇	14 ♏	58

29 SUNDAY

14:01 ◑ 6 ♏ 12

Moon Void of Course:
from 0:21 to 1:39 ♏

30 MONDAY

31 TUESDAY

Moon Void of Course:
from 6:03 to 14:00 ♐

The warlike party,
by the great Pontiff.
Who will subjugate
the frontiers of the Danube.
Those of the crooked cross...

Signs of the times.
Bishops give the
fascist salute to the
Duce. The crucifix
becomes the
"crooked cross" as
foreseen by the
French prophet.

AUGUST

*When weapons and plans are enclosed
in a fish (submarine) in 1996,
Out of it will come a man
who will then make war,
His fleet will have traveled
far across the sea
To appear at the Italian shore.*

LEO
Stone: Ruby
Metal: Gold
Color: Gold

Kings/Queens of the Zodiac, the Leos own the Royal elegance of those born at the top. Proud, vain and ambitious you love to be the center of attention and need constant admiration. Ruled by the Sun, your enthusiasm catches on easily and you are able to stimulate others. This, together with your fondness of dramatic display, could bring you to the stage or show business.

Honest and frank, you always mean what you say. Your speech is direct and simple. Generous and warm hearted you love teaching and caring for others. You make excellent doctors, educators, psychiatrist and politicians.

You are attracted to luxury and pleasure. You like to gamble with you money and spend it in things that will impress others, always surrounding yourself with the best of everything. When it

runs out, it won't be for long: the proud Leo will always find a way rather than admit that his wallet is empty.

Faith is part of your nature and whatever you believe in, you

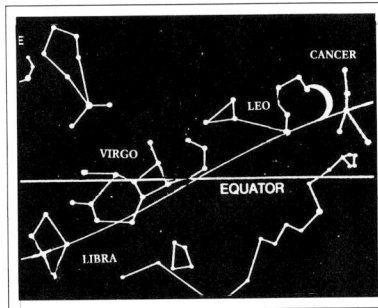

will stick to it with great sincerity, even with the most absurd doctrines.

Extremely romantic and passionate, you need to be proud of your love, but become quickly possessive and jealous. Beware of

the lion's paws when your Gemini friend talks too long to the stranger with beautiful blue eyes. At your worst you can be domineering, demanding, stubborn and rigid.

As a fixed sign, you are capable of long-sustained efforts. Your will-power and tenacity is unbeatable in carrying out your plans. You would rather be leaned on than lean on others. Commander at heart, you are at best when you exercise authority. Good organizer, you have a facility for leading big companies. You make an excellent executive, political leader, manager and salesperson.

With the Leo, the soul leads others, organizing and keeping the overview of the management. The attention to detail escape you and this is what you need to take care of as you approach Virgo, the following Sun sign of servitude.

THE ANTI-CHRIST

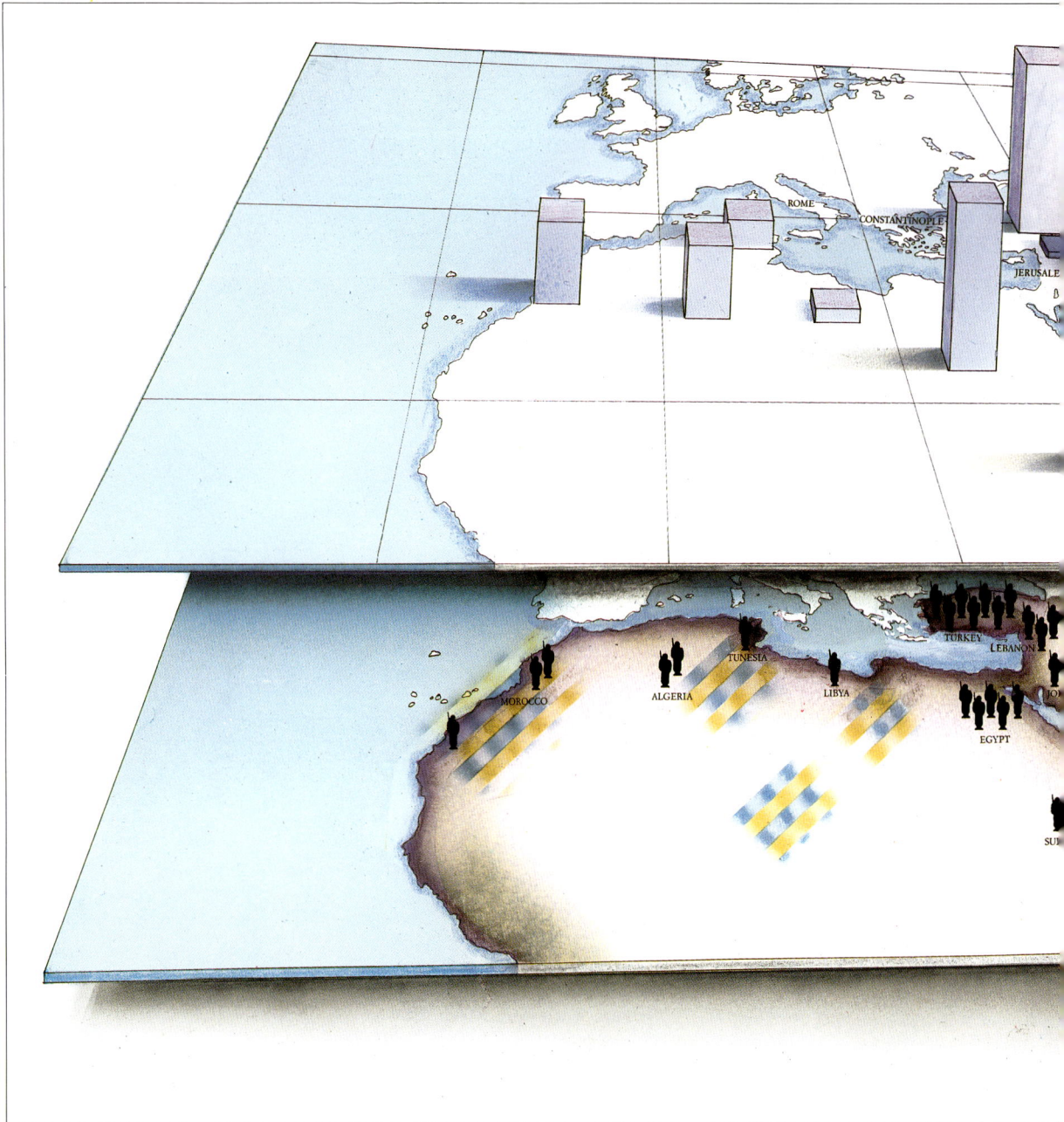

THE MIDDLE EAST
A RISING TIDE OF ISLAM IN
THE THEATER OF CONFLICT

Middle East & North Africa	Population (millions)	Armed Forces	Majority Fundamentalist Shi'ites	Ties with 2 Superpowers 1986
ALGERIA	21.7	130.000		
BAHRAIN	4	2.800	60%	
EGYPT	47.2	460.000		U.S.A.
IRAN	42.5	1.000.000	98%	
IRAQ	14.9	650.000	60%	U.S.S.R.
JORDAN	2.5	76.500		
KUWAIT	1.75	12.500		U.S.A.
LEBANON	2.7	20.300	77%	
LIBYA	3.5	73.000		U.S.S.R.
MOROCCO	23.4	144.000		U.S.A.
OMAN	1.6	21.500		
QUATAR	.27	6.000		
SAUDI ARABIA	10.4	51.000	15%	U.S.A.
SYRIA	10.4	362.000	5%	U.S.S.R.
SUDAN	23.25	58.000		
TUNESIA	7	35.000		
TURKEY	48.6	602.000		U.S.A.
U.A.E.	1.3	43.000		
YEMEN (north)	7.5	36.500		
YEMEN (south)	2.2	27.500		U.S.S.R.
Total	273.07	3.811.600		

■ Shi'ites ("following") are the cutting edge of Islam. In the West they are known as the Iranian storm troopers, the terrorists, the hijackers and the suicide bombers. Fanatic fundamentalists, they have up until recently been a minority group in every country but Iran, antipathetic to "immoral and corrupt" Western values.

▥ Sunnis ("custom"). The majority of Moslems are moderate, accepting the status quo and the modern Western influences, including some emancipation for women.

◈ Areas of conflict.

BAHRAIN QUATAR

OMAN

N (north)   YEMEN (south)

KHOMEINI

"The black and angry one," responsible for the fall of the Shah – "The great monarch of Persia" – and now perhaps a candidate for the third anti-christ.

KHADDAFI

During 1986, this contender for the third anti-christ in the prophet's quatrains, threatened the US and became involved in the Libyan confrontation in the Gulf of Sidra.

ABU ABBAS

This contender for the anti-christ is a shadowy and violent figure responsible for the Achille Lauro assault.

ABU NIDAL

"...the evil spirit that moves around only at night... causing them nightmares."

THE POLITICAL SCENE that was faced in *Nostradamus and the Millennium* can be seen as an interpretation of Nostradamus' view of our age in the light of its rebellious aspect. The prophet was much concerned with the religio-political position of mankind, and his term "anti-christ" reflects this position for in the 16th century anything that was against the state was also against God.

The whole Middle-East vs. US struggle has not really reduced since 1987 and we may yet see more activity in this area before the end of the millennium. Certainly, as far as Nostradamus was concerned, the fighting between the two sides has only just begun and is due to reach a peak in the early 1990s. This will be a matter of up-date from the Date Book that will appear in those years.

The main thrust of the quatrains surrounding the third anti-christ seem to be concerned with the results of nuclear fallout and the devastation that this will cause on Earth. We have already seen this fulfilled simply from the problems that have arrived on our door step insofar as the radio-active fallout level on this planet is already much higher than it was a decade ago.

The attempts during the latter part of the 1980s to reduce arms within the US and Soviet territories may be seen as a beginning of positive reaction to the fear engendered by the threat of nuclear war and we shall see how this unfolds during the 1990s.

But Nostradamus' real warning had much more to do with striking at the roots of the fear itself for it is this constant distrust that has created the blockade between the two countries in the first place.

How we can remedy fear in the hearts of mankind is yet to be discovered and may have much more to do with individual conditioning than national power struggling. It may also have to do with our choices of political leader – something that, at time of writing, is still proving to be a vital issue. Who knows whether the American people have chosen the right man or whether there is a right man at all.

1

WEDNESDAY

Moon Void of Course:
from 7:48 to 24:00

2

THURSDAY

Moon Void of Course:
from 0:00 to 24:00

3

FRIDAY

Moon Void of Course:
from 0:00 to 2:09 ♄

4

SATURDAY

*The third anti-christ very soon
annihilated
Twenty-seven years his bloody war
will last:
The heretics are dead, captives, exiled
Blood soaked human bodies, water,
and a reddened
icy rain covering the entire earth.*

LEO
Animal: Lion
Bird: Swan
Fish: Seal
Plant: Birch

5 SUNDAY

Moon Void of Course:
from 6:57 to 12:19 ≈

☉	12 ♌ 20
☿	8 ♍ 46
♀	19 ♋ 9
♂	15 ♈ 8
♃	27 ♋ 7
♄	20 ♑ 30 ℞
♅	6 ♑ 15 ℞
♆	12 ♑ 25 ℞
♇	15 ♏ 0

6 MONDAY

14:19 ○ 13 ≈ 52
14:13 Partial lunal eclipse

Moon Void of Course:
from 18:41 to 24:00

7 TUESDAY

Moon Void of Course:
from 0:00 to 19:54 ♓

8 WEDNESDAY

9 THURSDAY

Moon Void of Course:
from 22:03 to 24:00

10 FRIDAY

Moon Void of Course:
from 0:00 to 1:13 ♈

11 SATURDAY

Mabus will soon die, then will come
A horrible slaughter of people
and animals,
At once vengeance is revealed coming
from a hundred lands.
Thirst, and famine when the comet
will pass.

LEO
Rules the heart and back
Identity: The King/Queen
Keyword: Faith
Keynote: I will

SUNDAY

12

Moon Void of Course:
from 2:38 to 4:55 ☿

☉ 19 ♌ 3
☿ 16 ♍ 25
♀ 27 ♋ 40
♂ 19 ♅ 21
♃ 28 ♋ 39
♄ 20 ♉ 4 ℞
♅ 6 ♉ 3 ℞
♆ 12 ♉ 16 ℞
♇ 15 ♏ 3

MONDAY

13

15:54 ◑ 20 ♅ 38

TUESDAY

14

Moon Void of Course:
from 6:14 to 7:41 ♓

15 WEDNESDAY

Moon Void of Course:
from 22:05 to 24:00

16 THURSDAY

Moon Void of Course:
from 0:00 to 10:12 ♋

17 FRIDAY

18 SATURDAY

Moon Void of Course:
from 0:55 to 13:11 ♌

The quatrains that refer to the Soviet/US alliance that is due, according to the prophet, to take place in the late 1980s, are of particular significance, for even if they do not happen precisely at the time that we have interpreted, it seems clear today that we are growing close to something that would have seemed impossible only a decade ago. How long sighted was Nostradamus, that he could plot such an occurrence four hundred years before its time!

"The two will not remain allied for long,
Within the thirteen years they surrender to Barbare and
Iranian leaders
There will be such a loss on both sides, that one will
bless Petrus Romanus (the end of millennium
Pope)."

The main point of such an alliance might seem to be concerned with the power of two great nations standing against the Middle-Eastern threat – a development which arises yet again out of fear rather than intelligence so that Nostradamus' statement that such an alliance cannot last long would seem likely to be accurate. A marriage that has no love in it cannot survive.

And the result is then seen to be nuclear war followed by the much-mentioned "nuclear winter" – a time of darkness and depression that will fall upon the planet as a result of the failed efforts of our leaders.

But perhaps none of this will occur – we say – perhaps there will be some guardian angel watching over us that will alter the whole course of history in our favor. And it is, of course, exactly this idea which has got us into the situation we now find ourselves in.

One day the great powers
will become friends
Their great power will be seen
to increase.
The new land (America) will be at
the height of its power.
To the man of blood (the anti-christ)
the number is reported.

VIRGO
August 22nd – September 21st
Mutable – Earth
Negative – Interpersonal
Rules the 6th House
Ruled by Mercury

---

19 SUNDAY

☉	25 ♌ 46
☿	21 ♍ 41
♀	6 ♌ 13
♂	23 ♑ 23
♃	0 ♌ 9
♄	19 ♑ 40 ℞
♅	5 ♑ 54 ℞
♆	12 ♑ 8 ℞
♇	15 ♏ 8

---

20 MONDAY

12:39 ● 27 ♌ 15

Moon Void of Course:
from 12:39 to 17:33 ♍

---

21 TUESDAY

22 WEDNESDAY

Moon Void of Course:
from 15:41 to 24:00

23 THURSDAY

Moon Void of Course:
from 0:00 to 0:17 ♎

24 FRIDAY

Moon Void of Course:
from 13:14 to 24:00

25 SATURDAY

Moon Void of Course:
from 0:00 to 9:56 ♏

*The two will not remain
allied for long,
Within the thirteen years they
surrender to Barbare
and Iranian leaders
There will be such a loss on both
sides,
that one will bless Petrus Romanus.*

VIRGO
Mercury in exaltation
Saturn strong
Neptune in detriment
Venus in fall

26 SUNDAY

☉	2 ♍ 31
☿	23 ♍ 34 ℞
♀	14 ♌ 47
♂	27 ♉ 11
♃	1 ♌ 37
♄	19 ♉ 20 ℞
♅	5 ♉ 46 ℞
♆	12 ♉ 1 ℞
♇	15 ♏ 14

27 MONDAY

Moon Void of Course:
from 18:07 to 21:57 ♐

28 TUESDAY

7:34 ◑ 4 ♐ 45

29 WEDNESDAY

Moon Void of Course:
from 19:45 to 24:00

30 THURSDAY

Moon Void of Course:
from 0:00 to 10:23 ♉

31 FRIDAY

SEPTEMBER

*A horrible war which is being
prepared in the west,
The following year the pestilence
will come,
So very horrible that young nor old,
nor animal (may survive).
Blood fire Mercury Mars Jupiter
in France.*

VIRGO
Stone: Onyx
Metal: Mercury
Color: Ocher and browns

Striving for perfection, the reserved Virgo has the reputation of being almost maniacal for detail. Critical and analyzing you see the faults in everything around you. You want to be perfect and you want the world to be perfect, you know your imperfections and this is why it is so annoying to you hearing from someone that you have done something wrong when you've already spent the last half hour beating yourself about it.

You have inherited the quick mind, intelligence and the matter of fact qualities of Mercury, as well as his nervousness, that you conceal along with your worries behind a straight and worldly facade. Your shrewd and diplomatic nature makes you an ingenious businessmen, although you can do very well at the office among the papers and the files. Your critical and analytical mind makes you efficient in an investigating and research field. You are good at saving money and will not spend it in frivolous things.

Ruled by the Earth element you are conscientious, punctual and reliable. Hard worker and practical, you have the great ability to concentrate on details. When you take a task at hand, you will only let it go if it is completed and perfected to the absolute minute detail, sometimes at the cost of many frustrations. Virgo being the sign of services, you willingly do people's favors, but because you despise being dependent on others, you don't accept so easily theirs.

Virgo rules the bowels and your worrying and nervous nature may affect this area if you are not careful, but since you have very precise ideas about health and a natural fascination for food, one of your medical remedies or diets will probably do the trick.

In general you are cool with your body and slow to decide when it comes to romance. First you want to find the perfect partner and be sure it is going to be a lifelong affair before you commit yourself. You would happily remain as a bachelor rather than be with someone you see as stupid, careless or unreliable, characteristics which can make you feel quite irritable when you are confronted by them.

Going towards Libra, the Virgo has to learn about the justice and love of his following Sun sign.

BLOOD PLAGUE

Louis Pasteur, pioneer of immunology and micro-biology, was commented on by Nostradamus, three hundred and thirty-three years earlier.

In occult symbolism, the sword stands for the male phallus.

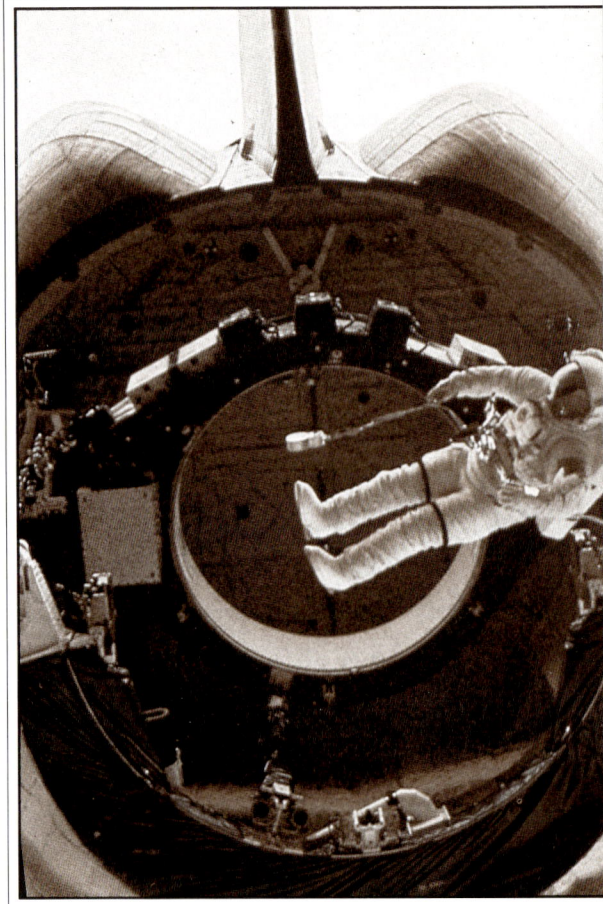

NOSTRADAMUS' INTEREST and knowledge surrounding disease and especially plague, would have drawn his attention to our present AIDS virus. His quatrains are painfully specific about the disease with projections of the rate of growth of the disease during the latter part of this millennium which might have been considered dramatic only a few years ago, but which are quickly proving to be accurate as the decade of the 80s departs into history.

Current medical research shows AIDS to be primarily spread through anal intercourse and any other blood-on-blood and sperm-on-blood contact, making the homosexual community the highest risk group. Second highest come drug addicts sharing needles, hemophiliacs and others needing blood products and Haitians who have carried the disease to the west from Africa.

His vision that some half of the world will be infected during the 1990s is still a terrifying prospect but when we look at the potential statistics in the US right now it is clear that we cannot discount the possibility that nearly half of America is already, without knowing, infected by AIDS.

Much of the power of Nostradamus' prophecies lies in their rather negative and doom-ridden quality, but there is also a strong positive aspect to his work which runs alongside the darkness.

Both the US and the USSR plan space satellites for the mid to late 1990s which will be orbiting at the appropriate distance from Earth and the recent Challenger disaster is likely to help the Soviets launch their "Samarobrin" first.
Whoever succeeds in the scientific exploration of "space-grown" crystals, may produce the cure for AIDS so much sought today.

1

SATURDAY

Moon Void of Course:
from 4:25 to 20:51 ♒

2

SUNDAY

☉	9	♍ 17
☿	20	♍ 51 ℞
♀	23	♌ 24
♂	0	♓ 45
♃	3	♌ 2
♄	19	♉ 4 ℞
♅	5	♉ 40 ℞
♆	11	♉ 56 ℞
♇	15	♏ 22

3

MONDAY

Moon Void of Course:
from 20:20 to 24:00

4

TUESDAY

Moon Void of Course:
from 0:00 to 4:06 ♓

5

WEDNESDAY

1:46 ○ 12 ♓ 15

Moon Void of Course:
from 13:25 to 24:00

6

THURSDAY

Moon Void of Course:
from 0:00 to 8:23 ♈

7

FRIDAY

Moon Void of Course:
from 16:20 to 24:00

8

SATURDAY

Moon Void of Course:
from 0:00 to 10:55 ♉

*The lost thing, hidden for
many centuries, is discovered.
Pasteur will be honored as a demigod.
This happens when the moon completes
her great cycle.
He will be dishonored
by other rumors.*

VIRGO
Animal: Fox
Bird: Crane and stork
Fish: Chub
Plant: Carrot and beet

9 SUNDAY

Moon Void of Course:
from 18:24 to 24:00

☉ 16 ♍ 4
☿ 14 ♍ 27 ℞
♀ 2 ♍ 3
♂ 4 ♓ 2
♃ 4 ♌ 25
♄ 18 ♉ 52 ℞
♅ 5 ♉ 37 ℞
♆ 11 ♉ 52 ℞
♇ 15 ♏ 32

10 MONDAY

Moon Void of Course:
from 0:00 to 13:05 ♓

11 TUESDAY

20:53 ◑ 18 ♓ 51
Moon Void of Course:
from 20:53 to 24:00

12 WEDNESDAY

Moon Void of Course:
from 0:00 to 15:53 ♋

13 THURSDAY

14 FRIDAY

Moon Void of Course:
from 4:19 to 19:52 ♌

15 SATURDAY

Moon Void of Course:
from 23:39 to 24:00

*...Swords damp with blood from
distant lands.
A very great plague will come
with a great scab.
Relief near but the remedies far away.*

VIRGO
Rules the intestines
Identity: The Analyst
Keyword: Service
Keynote: I analyze

16 SUNDAY

Moon Void of Course:
from 0:00 to 24:00

☉ 22 ♍ 53
☿ 9 ♍ 46 ℞
♀ 10 ♍ 43
♂ 6 ♓ 59
♃ 5 ♌ 43
♄ 18 ♑ 45 ℞
♅ 5 ♑ 36
♆ 11 ♑ 49 ℞
♇ 15 ♏ 43

17 MONDAY

Moon Void of Course:
from 0:00 to 1:19 ♍

18 TUESDAY

19

WEDNESDAY

0:46 ● 25 ♍ 50

Moon Void of Course:
from 0:46 to 8:34 ♎

20

THURSDAY

Moon Void of Course:
from 20:09 to 24:00

21

FRIDAY

Moon Void of Course:
from 0:00 to 18:06 ♏

22

SATURDAY

This light side of Nostrada-mus comes in the form of an aware-ness of the consciousness of man-kind.

Consciousness as an element of man has been around for thou-sands of years and Nostradamus would have been closer to it's phil-osophies and understandings than perhaps we are today. The essence of consciousness within the 16th century was closely allied, like everything else, with religion. The Prophet's experiences with the Catholic Inquisition were not happy, as he was constantly being hounded by the Cardinals because of their belief that he was connec-ted with black magic practices and witchcraft – a superstition that prevailed during this and many other times in history. We have now entered, once again, an age which may be more concerned with un-reason. We call it The New Age or the era of Human Po-tential and Nostradamus would have been much at home in such a time. For running alongside the death and disaster of our age there is a new rising of the consciousness

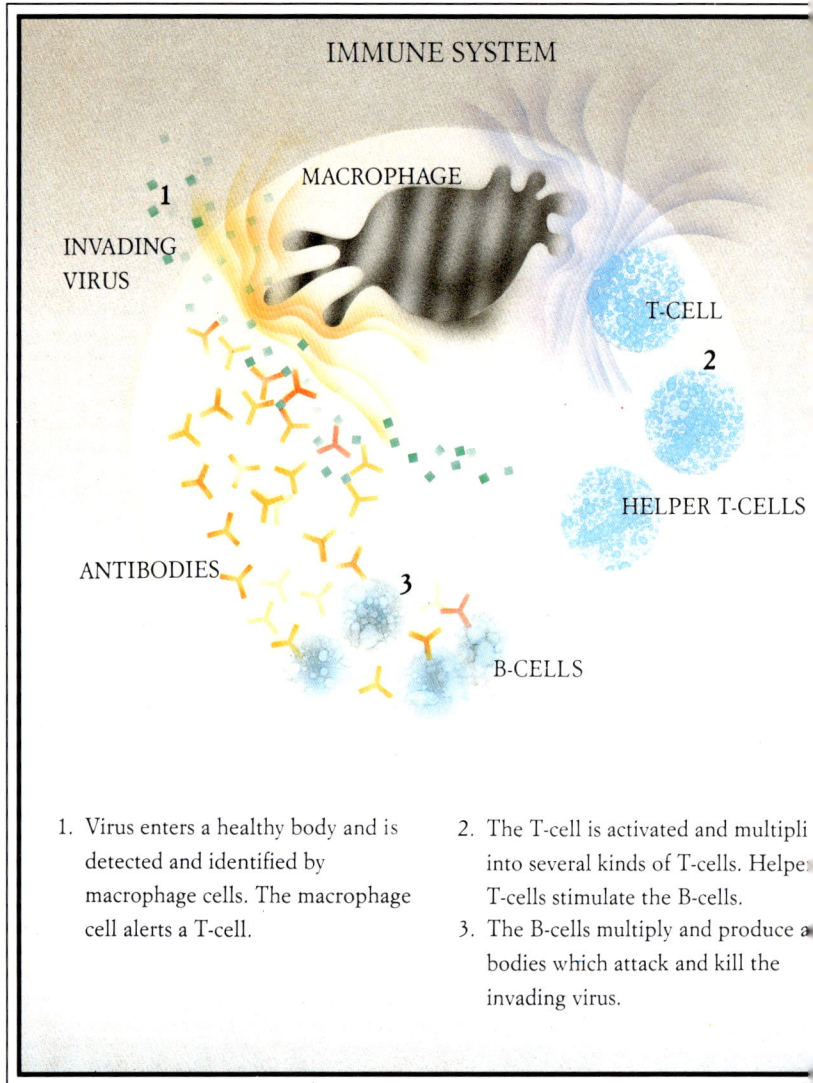

IMMUNE SYSTEM

1. Virus enters a healthy body and is detected and identified by macrophage cells. The macrophage cell alerts a T-cell.

2. The T-cell is activated and multipli into several kinds of T-cells. Helpe T-cells stimulate the B-cells.

3. The B-cells multiply and produce a bodies which attack and kill the invading virus.

"...SWORDS WET WITH BLOOD FROM DISTAN

AIDS VIRUS ATTACK

MACROPHAGE

INVADING
AIDS-VIRUS

T-CELL

1

2

AIDS-VIRUS
GROWING IN T-CELLS

MALIGNANT T-CELLS PRODUCE
MORE AIDS-VIRUS

When the AIDS-virus attacks it infects the helper T-cells. It blocks their ability to detect alien substances and then changes the T-cells into AIDS-virus factories.

2. Because the T-cells no longer perform their role of fighting infections the invading viruses encounter no resistance and move throughout the body. The damaged T-cells produce more AIDS-viruses which invade more T-cells.

NDS, A VERY GREAT PLAGUE WILL COME..."

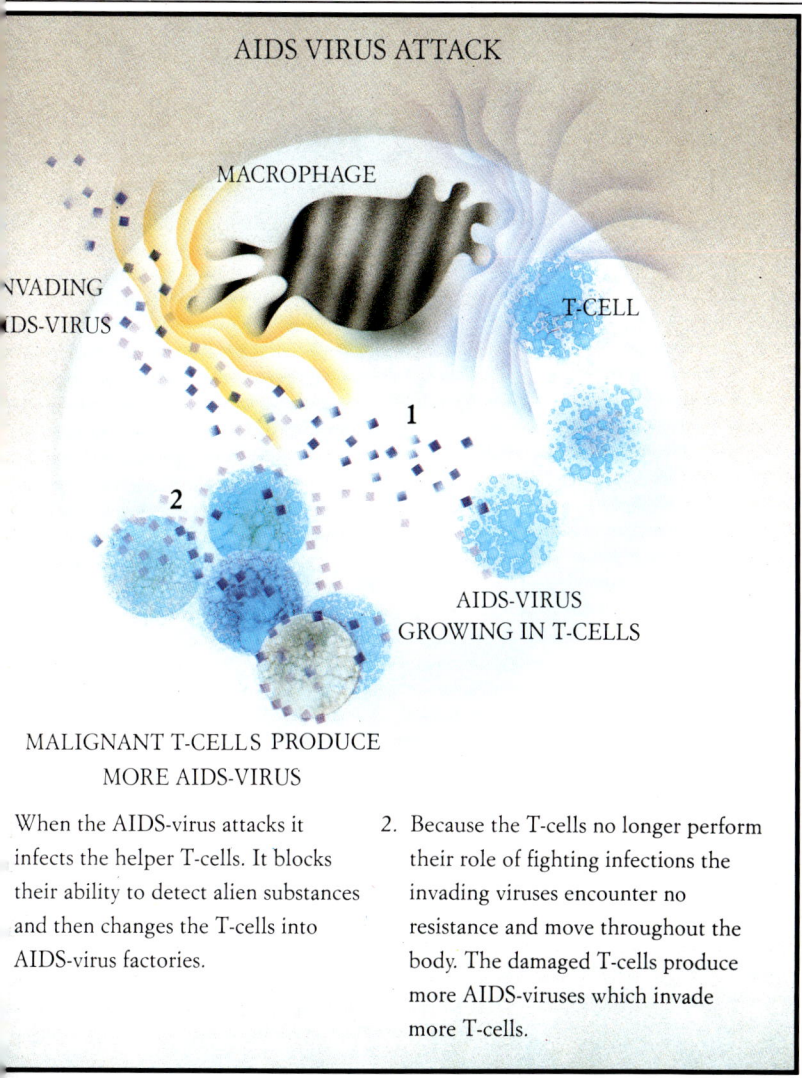

of individuals to the way the world works and what our place is within it.

Nostradamus' basic message in relation to consciousness was that if we could raise our level of awareness and intelligence, all the problems that we now face would be easily solved. Today still, many would call this naive idealism, and prefer to struggle with the complexity of life as it presently remains. But Nostradamus was very much an idealist and beside from his very practical and down-to-earth predictions he also projected times of beauty and harmony on Earth.

For example, during the early 21st century he foresees a long period of peace in which it becomes possible for the human race to establish a galactic community. The foundation for this "thousand years of peace" is a merging of science and religion that he foresees happening at this time.

The merging of science and religion would be more likely to occur once both the scientist and the priest or theologian became

A great famine through
a pestilent wave.
(It) will extend its rain over
the length of the arctic pole,
Samarobrin, one hundred leagues
from the hemisphere,
They shall live without law,
exempt from politics.

LIBRA
September 22nd – October 22nd
Cardinal – Air
Positive – Interpersonal
Rules the 7th House
Ruled by Venus

☉	29 ♍	43
☿	11 ♍	57
♀	19 ♍	24
♂	9 ♓	32
♃	6 ♌	58
♄	18 ♉	42
♅	5 ♉	38
♆	11 ♉	48
♇	15 ♏	55

23 SUNDAY

Moon Void of Course:
from 9:32 to 24:00

24 MONDAY

Moon Void of Course:
from 0:00 to 5:52 ♐

25 TUESDAY

26 WEDNESDAY

Moon Void of Course:
from 5:18 to 18:36 ♑

27 THURSDAY

2:06 ◑ 3 ♑ 43

28 FRIDAY

Moon Void of Course:
from 23:50 to 24:00

29 SATURDAY

Moon Void of Course:
from 0:00 to 5:54 ♒

In the feeble lists,
great calamity through America...
plague...Mercury in Sagittarius,
Saturn warning.

LIBRA
Saturn in exaltation
Jupiter strong
Mars in detriment
Sun in fall

SUNDAY

30

Moon Void of Course:
from 12:27 to 24:00

☉	6 ♎	35
☿	20 ♍	32
♀	28 ♍	7
♂	11 ♓	38
♃	8 ♌	9
♄	18 ♉	45
♅	5 ♉	42
♆	11 ♉	49
♇	16 ♏	8

Nostradamus had to deal with a common superstition that armies of demons and angels descended from the skies to strike plague victims with invisible arrows and supernatural swords. The word "swords" might therefore have been a poetic analogy for the spread of a plague.

familiar with one another's work and this seems today to be happening. With publications such as *The Tao of Physics* by Fritjof Capra, *The Spectrum of Consciousness* by Ken Wilbur, we come closer and closer to merging the ideas of the precise and the philosophical and perhaps this gentle beginning will increase during the New Age where all things are once again being questioned.

Some of the better known scientists still insist that they are close to finding a Unified Theory of the whole universe while philosophers of the Eastern tradition still insist that the only Unified Theory of the universe is that there is no Unified theory – the universe simply keeps changing and to tie it down to a fixed theory is ridiculous.

A merging of two such diverse concepts seems unlikely at this moment, but more extreme differences have been resolved in the past.

During the next month, we shall be looking at how mother nature might resolve these differences for us if we refuse to take the responsibility ourselves.

And one of her methods may be to teach us that we are all already joined with her in her effort to keep a balance on this delicate and powerful planet.

OCTOBER

LIBRA
Stone: Sapphire
Metal: Copper
Color: Pink and light green

Up and down, left and right, as an airy Libran you are constantly weighing the possibilities. A bit more here, a bit less there, constantly trying to equalize the scales in search of harmony and peace. Before embarking on a decision, you take the situation apart, calculate the pros and cons and will not decide until you have examined all the possibilities. At first seeming hesitant and uncertain, once decided, you will not go back an inch and even become as stubborn as the Aries.

This ability to dissect every angle of a situation will make you the best at an argument. In fact, anyone who starts arguing with a Libra should know that he has already lost.

Your curiosity is insatiable, you watch and compare every detail of other peoples affairs, always searching to draw conclusions.

You love gossips and scandals, but only as long as you are not involved in it and will go to great extent to avoid being mixed up in any conflict. In the affairs of the heart, this habit of taking things apart will make you disappointed in people and when, in some Libran, this habit becomes exaggerated, it can drive anyone mad... or away.

You hate disorder, noise and ugliness as well as extremities and exaggeration and get easily annoyed when confronted by them. Although you dislike show-offs and dramatic displays of anger and passion you can become quite bitter yourself when pushed to the extreme. Because you need harmonious and pleasant surroundings, you often keep your real feelings bottled up.

Your Venusian charm is irresistible: a soft voice, gentle features and a wonderful smile. Refined, perceptive and sensitive you are a lover of beauty and pleasure. Always dressed in the best fashions, you delight in parties and social events. To those born in the sign of Libra, love and relationships will be very important. You like poetry, music and painting and are also inclined towards law and higher professions.

In the soul's search for peace and harmony as it goes through Libra, it has lost the depth and single pointedness that the Scorpio can have. In its longing for justice, the Libra needs to touch not only the logic and the esthetics but also acquire the depth and the ability to concentrate on the following Sun sign. By bringing the harmony inside, rather than looking for it outside, the Libra could achieve what he longs for: bringing peace into his innermost being.

EARTH STRIKES BACK

Mexico earthquake – 1985.

THE CONCEPT OF homeostasis is one that has been familiar to medicine for some time. It explains how the body is able to maintain certain physical and chemical balances through glands and hormone producing organs that keep us constantly at the same temperature, the blood flowing at a certain rate and many other biological processes stable.

It is only, however, during the latter part of this century that science has arrived at the conclusion that the whole planet Earth operates in the same way. This is evidenced, for example, by the fact that the oxygen in the air is always at the same relative percentage to other gases – 21% and the sea contains always the same 3.5% of salt – never varying, however much salt washes into it, the same amount is deposited onto the land.

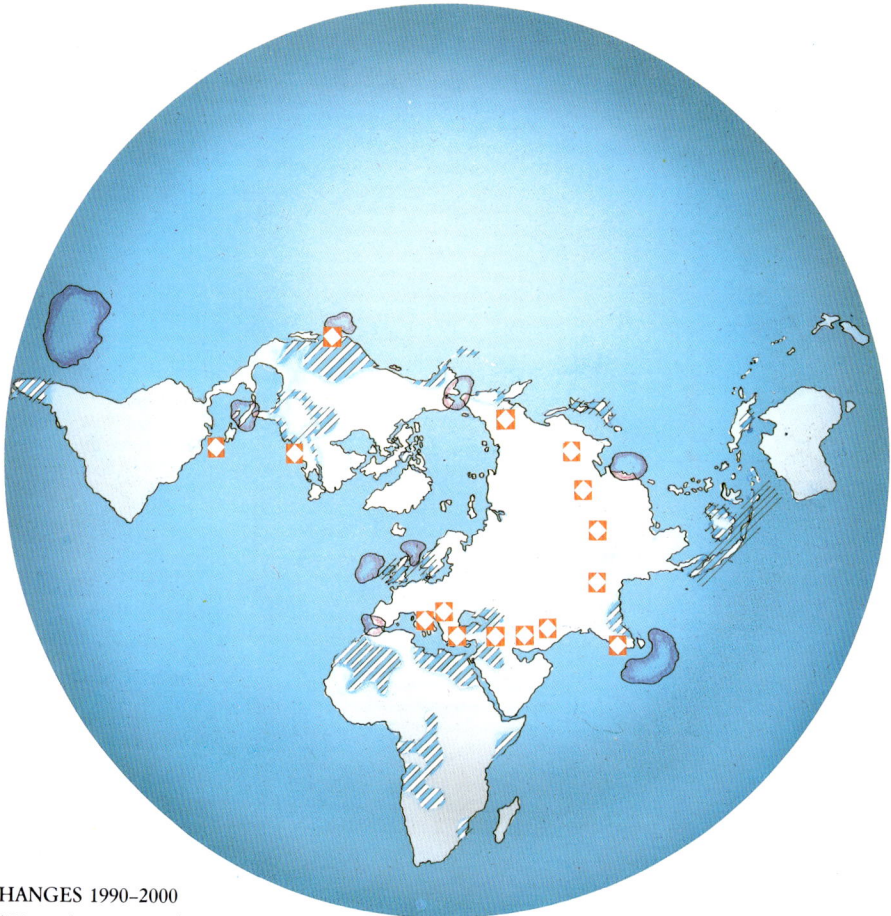

MAJOR EARTH CHANGES 1990–2000

Modern psychics and Nostradamus agree that the first in a chain of superquakes will begin in or near the Indian sub-continent. A sudden escalation of quakes will occur in the late 1980's, first flooding the west coast of India and then Japan, then moving westward on the Earth's crust causing record eruptions of Mt. Etna in Sicily and Vesuvius in Italy. North and west European coastlines are violently altered, bringing the Atlantic to Paris and London from the west. Next comes the long awaited superquake in the San Andreas fault which will rock the west coast of America. Sea water will flood into the southern californian deserts from the gulf of

PROJECTED BY PROPHETS AND PSYCHICS

EARTHQUAKE ◈ AREAS

NEW ▢ LAND

NEW ▨ COASTLINE

California as the west coast breaks away from the mainland. By the mid-1990's a second wave of superquakes is generally foreseen. By then the western United States will have vanished or broken up into islands. East Africa will split into three pieces. South America and Tierra del Fuego also split apart. New York City and Florida will be flooded as new continent-sized islands rise off the Carribean, the submerged coast of Southern California and the South Pacific. New Zealand, Australia, Siberia, Northern Canada, New Mexico and Virginia in the United States, are seen by modern psychics as safe areas.

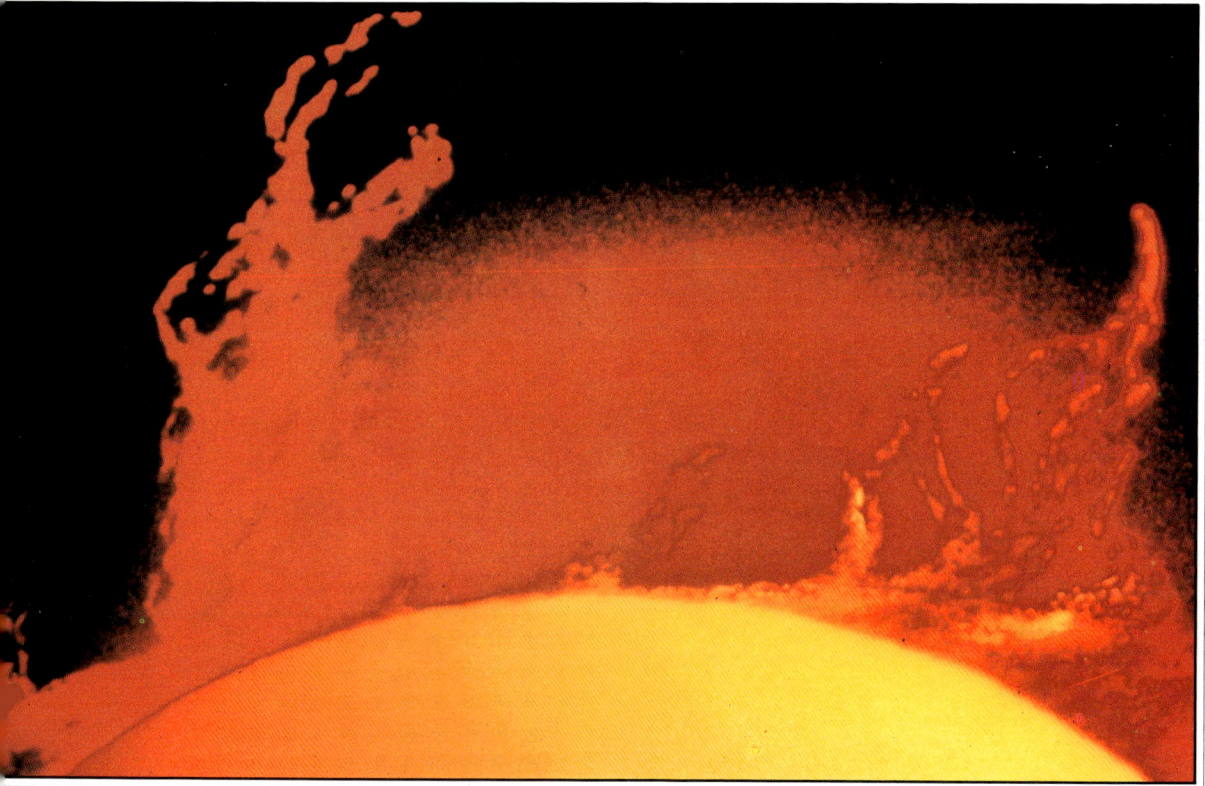

Solar Flares.
Scientists have traced the regularity of sun spot activity over the last billion years and relate it to twenty years cycles which coincide with periods of drought such as the famous "Dust bowl" drought in the American farming belt during the 1930s. Sun spot activity is now entering a new phase which will continue through until the year 2000.

According to Nostradamus, Africa is now and in the near future the greatest risk area for drought and famine. This natural disaster area began its serious famines in the past three years (marked brown) and stands at risk again in 1987, exactly as the prophet predicted.

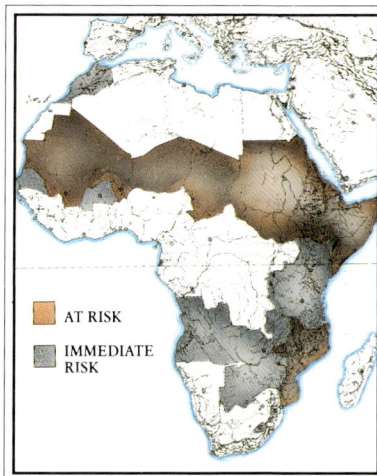

AT RISK

IMMEDIATE RISK

Nostradamus often used the number of his quatrains to signify the year of his predictions and if this is so we can expect a world drought by July 1998. The greenhouse effect may disrupt weather patterns and move climate conditions needed to grow grain hundreds of miles north from where they are now.

Mt. Pele.
The work of a volcano – in 1902 Mount Pele erupted over Martinique and literally leveled the city. Nature's power to destroy is far greater than man's.

1 MONDAY

Moon Void of Course:
from 0:00 to 13:42 ♓

2 TUESDAY

3

WEDNESDAY

Moon Void of Course:
from 11:09 to 17:42 ♈

4

THURSDAY

12:02 ○ 11 ♈ 0

5

FRIDAY

Moon Void of Course:
from 0:53 to 19:06 ♀

6

SATURDAY

The great famine which
I sense approaching
will often turn (up in various places)
then become universal:
It will be so vast and long lasting
That (people) will grab roots from
the trees and children from the breast.

LIBRA
Animal: Butterfly
Bird: Dove
Fish: Dolphin and whale
Plant: Sweet pea and rose

7

SUNDAY

Moon Void of Course:
from 1:40 to 19:47 ♓

☉	13 ♎	28
☿	2 ♎	12
♀	6 ♎	51
♂	13 ♓	14
♃	9 ♌	14
♄	18 ♉	52
♅	5 ♉	49
♆	11 ♉	51
♇	16 ♏	23

8

MONDAY

Moon Void of Course:
from 20:57 to 24:00

9

TUESDAY

Moon Void of Course:
from 0:00 to 21:29 ♋

10 WEDNESDAY

11 THURSDAY

3:31 ◐ 17 ♋ 34

Moon Void of Course:
from 5:58 to 24:00

12 FRIDAY

Moon Void of Course:
from 0:00 to 1:16 ♌

13 SATURDAY

Moon Void of Course:
from 12:57 to 24:00

*Earth shaking fire from
the center of the Earth
Will cause the towers around the
New City to shake:
Two great rocks will war
for a long time,
And then Arethus shall color
a new river red.*

LIBRA
Rules kidneys
Identity: The Lover
Keyword: Harmony
Keynote: I relate

14 SUNDAY

Moon Void of Course:
from 0:00 to 7:21 ♍

☉	20 ♎	23
☿	14 ♎	30
♀	15 ♎	36
♂	14 ♓	14
♃	10 ♌	13
♄	19 ♉	4
♅	5 ♉	58
♆	11 ♉	55
♇	16 ♏	38

15 MONDAY

Moon Void of Course:
from 18:53 to 24:00

16 TUESDAY

Moon Void of Course:
from 0:00 to 15:26 ♎

17 WEDNESDAY

18 THURSDAY

15:37 ● 25 ♎ 0
Moon Void of Course:
from 15:37 to 24:00

19 FRIDAY

Moon Void of Course:
from 0:00 to 1:24 ♏

20 SATURDAY

Moon Void of Course:
from 15:42 to 24:00

Mexico 1985

This global homeostasis was known to Nostradamus in the 16th century, long, long before science caught up with it. The prophet was completely aware that everything man does to his world affects the balance of these finely adjusted factors and foresaw that if we behaved as we have been doing this century; exploding bombs, cutting down forests and destroying natural life, for long enough we would eventually suffer the consequences.

He saw it in very simple terms – that if we shifted this natural balance then nature, or Earth herself, would strike back at us with the other side of the game – storms, earthquakes, volcanoes, shifts in the Earth's plates, and that these changes would have to happen in order for nature to readjust her position and make the balance reoccur.

During the next one and half decades before the end of the millennium we are likely to see more of such Mother Earth behavior – unless we make changes ourselves.

A great kingdom will remain desolate,
Near the Ebro they will be gathered
in assemblies.
The Pyreness mountains will
console him
When in May there are
great earthquakes.

SCORPIO
October 23rd – November 21st
Fixed – Water
Negative – Interpersonal
Rules the 8th House
Ruled by Pluto

21 SUNDAY

Moon Void of Course:
from 0:00 to 13:09 ⚹

☉	27 ♎ 20
☿	26 ♎ 32
♀	24 ♎ 22
♂	14 ♓ 34 ℞
♃	11 ♌ 6
♄	19 ♉ 20
♅	6 ♑ 9
♆	12 ♑ 0
♇	16 ♏ 54

22 MONDAY

23 TUESDAY

Moon Void of Course:
from 22:01 to 24:00

24
WEDNESDAY

Moon Void of Course:
from 0:00 to 2:03 ♉

25
THURSDAY

Moon Void of Course:
from 17:32 to 24:00

26
FRIDAY

20:26 ◑ 3 ♒ 10
Moon Void of Course:
from 0:00 to 14:14 ♒

27
SATURDAY

Moon Void of Course:
from 23:25 to 24:00

28 SUNDAY

Moon Void of Course:
from 0:00 to 23:22 ♓

☉	4	♏ 19
☿	8	♏ 5
♀	3	♏ 8
♂	14	♓ 11 ℞
♃	11	♌ 52
♄	19	♉ 41
♅	6	♉ 23
♆	12	♉ 7
♇	17	♏ 10

29 MONDAY

30 TUESDAY

Moon Void of Course:
from 10:47 to 24:00

31 WEDNESDAY

Moon Void of Course:
from 0:00 to 4:14 ♈

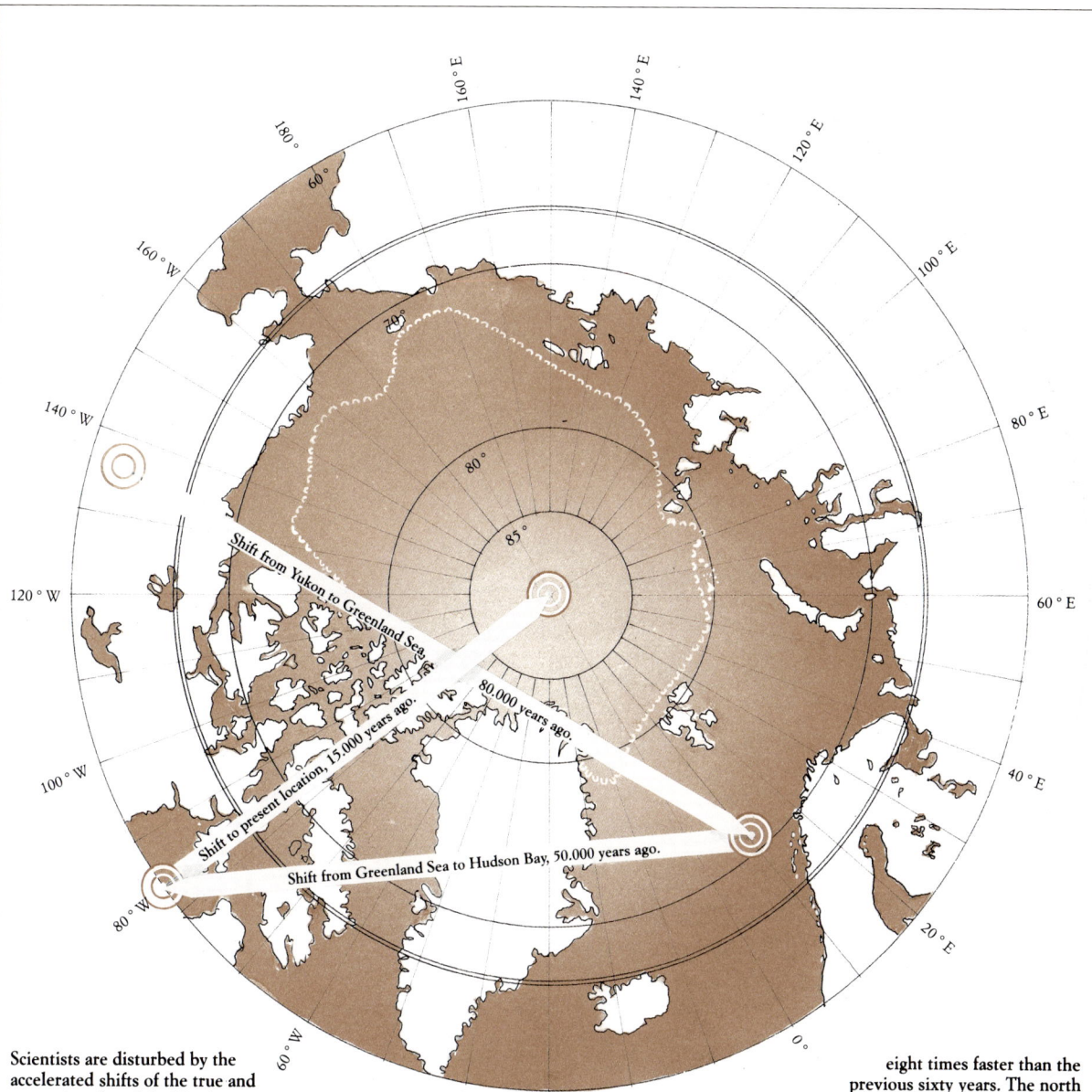

Shift from Yukon to Greenland Sea

Shift to present location, 15,000 years ago.

80,000 years ago.

Shift from Greenland Sea to Hudson Bay, 50,000 years ago.

Scientists are disturbed by the accelerated shifts of the true and magnetic poles of the Earth in recent times. Leading experts like Hapgood believe we are already seeing a new axis shift in progress. The north pole has moved ten feet between 1960 and 1968 – eight times faster than the previous sixty years. The north magnetic pole has shifted four hundred and eighty times to the northwest between 1931 and 1984 while the south magnetic pole is racing into the Indian Ocean.

NOVEMBER

*Many people will want
to come to terms
With the great world leaders who
will bring war upon them:
The political leaders will not want
to hear anything of their message,
Alas! If God does not send peace
to the Earth.*

SCORPIO
Uranus in exaltation
Sun strong
Venus in detriment
Moon in fall

Magnetic, intense and mysterious, the Scorpio possesses the hypnotic powers over others. You silently watch people with your deeply penetrating eyes as if you can read their life on the spot. Most likely you can. You see every detail in everybody's life, always updated with the gossips. Because you are so good at unraveling the life of other people you would make very good detectives. In fact, Scorpio rules investigating agencies.

On the other hand, it is hard to pin point you: you are suspicious, skeptical, cautious and secretive. No one gets to really know you, you keep your innermost feelings to yourself in the fear that someone may use them against you. You are capable of withstanding the most delicate situations without showing the slightest emotion.

Determined, shrewd and tenacious, you need to be total in whatever you do. Either you go fully into something or you don't do it at all. When you say or do something you mean it. It is very important for you to have a cause to devote yourself to or a creative outlet, otherwise those powerful energies manifest themselves in their most negative traits: resentfulness, vengeful, self hatred and manipulation.

You hate taking orders, in fact, you like to dominate others. Secretly ambitious, you will wait for the chance to move ahead towards your goal.

When it comes to sex you are either a saint or a sinner: you can be ardent, passionate, eager to fulfill your needs, possessive and possessed, even perverted like only a Scorpio can be. On the other hand, you can be very dogmatic, putting yourself to the rule and sticking to it, in a self-denying way. Many Scorpios have chosen the path of celibacy.

You are interested in the occult, religion, psychology life and death. Not only solving the outer mysteries fascinates you, but also the inner ones.

When the soul passes the Sun sign of Scorpio, it touches the deepest of the human heart. Very potent transforming energies are at work, but the understanding of them is not yet complete. Scorpi through following an ideal will learn how to take things lightly and to forgive others like his following Sun sign.

A NEW AWAKENING

A new turn comes at the end of this millennium. One of Nostradamus' main clues to the man who will make this "turn" of the "wheel" comes in the form of the symbol of birds flying in the sky.

THE CHAPTER IN *Nostradamus and the Millennium* that covered the New Awakening outlined the quatrains which are concerned with a new religious leader who will emerge once the old Catholic Church has disappeared.

In order to bring a perspective to the possible candidates for this position in the future this chapter was concerned to show each of the living Masters that we are living with today. The general conclusion of the book was that, according to the interpretations of the quatrains, the most likely candidate was Bhagwan Shree Rajneesh, a man who has seen much controversy in the last decade especially in America where he suffered the wrong side of the US government and eventually was forced to leave the new commune that had been set up in the State of Oregon in order that he might be with his disciples.

The amount of anger and criticism he received after one of his leading disciples broke the law was unprecedented in recent history and it was unfortunate that the experiment died then and there, at least insofar as the US people were concerned.

But the experiment has con-

J. KRISHNAMURTI

MEHER BABA

YOGANANDA

tinued elsewhere in the world – in India, where a new commune is flourishing despite many attempts by the US government and the Indian authorities to stop it.

It seems that after the Oregon commune, named Rajneeshpuram, broke up, Bhagwan Shree Rajneesh was thereafter refused access to almost all countries around the world and eventually was forced to return to India, his native country, where he has been ever since.

Though there is no sound proof of it, many of his disciples believe that their Master was refused access to countries because of pressure put on the governments by the US authorities – a sad state if true, for in a nation which

"God bless Mommy, God bless Daddy, and God bless all the other fanatical lunatics who are subverting my religious freedom with their archaic jargon."

speaks much of the freedom of individuals, such acts would amount to a direct breach of human rights.

But the saddest of all aspects of this story is the fact that few Americans now know anything about

what Rajneesh has to tell the world – in fact probably Nostradamus knew more!

His philosophy of love and understanding stands as one of great simplicity and would seem an unlikely one to upset any organization, save perhaps for the established religions.

According to the numerous quatrains within Nostradamus' "The Centuries," it is hard to dispute that Rajneesh fits the story of the future leader of a world religion which is due to arrive sometime very soon.

The prophecies even point to a man who is taken in chains and imprisoned, flown across the world with followers who wear red. Bhagwan's disciples dressed

THE CLUES:	EAST	HERMES	OUTLAWED	RED	MARS	MOON	TRAVELS	BIRD
VISIONARIES:								
YOGANANDA	*			*	*		*	
BABA	*							
PRABHUPADA	*		*	*				
HUBBARD			*					
KRISHNAMURTI	*	*		*	*		*	
SAI BABA	*			*				
MOON	*		*			*	*	
RAJNEESH	*	*	*	*	*	*	*	*
YOGI	*	*	*				*	
FREE JOHN		*	*			*	*	

BHAGWAN SHREE RAJNEESH

DA FREE JOHN

"The teacher is considered an outlaw" Bhagwan Shree Rajneesh in chains in America 1985.

in orange and red clothes for th
first 12 years of their disciplehoo
and only after the event in Americ
did he suggest that they drop th
colors. His time in jail in Americ
was spent in chains and after hi
departure he spent months flyin
around the world attempting t
find a home elsewhere, all the tim
talking to people in every countr
about his philosophy of love an
good will.

There are a number of livin
Masters alive today – Da Fre
John, U.G. Krishnamurti, Mahar
shi Mahesh Yogi, but none of the
appear to have the power and pre
ence of Rajneesh. And in an
event, few or none of Nostrad
mus' quatrains make any direct re
ference to them at all.

If we believe that Nostrad
mus had any foresight whatever i
these or other matters, then w
might wish to look once more
this man Rajneesh and see if
haps the prejudices and fears of th
American authorities outweighe
their good sense. If perhaps the
managed to throw away an oppo
tunity to welcome a Master wh

*A man will be charged with destroying
the temples and religions altered
by fantasy.
He will harm the rocks rather
than the living.
Ears filled with ornate speeches.*

SCORPIO
Stone: Garnet
Metal: Iron
Color: Dark red

1 THURSDAY

Moon Void of Course:
from 13:19 to 24:00

2 FRIDAY

21:48 ○ 10 ☿ 13

Moon Void of Course:
from 0:00 to 5:31 ☿

3 SATURDAY

Moon Void of Course:
from 13:25 to 24:00

He will appear in Asia (and be)
at home in Europe...
The man from the East will
come out of his seat
Passing across the Appenines
to see France
He will fly through the sky...

SCORPIO
Animal: Scorpion and snake
Bird: Hawk
Fish: Scorpion fish
Plant: Pine

4 SUNDAY

Moon Void of Course:
from 0:00 to 5:06 ♓

☉ 11 ♏ 18
☿ 19 ♏ 12
♀ 11 ♏ 54
♂ 13 ♓ 5 ℞
♃ 12 ♌ 30
♄ 20 ♑ 7
♅ 6 ♑ 39
♆ 12 ♑ 16
♇ 17 ♏ 27

5 MONDAY

Moon Void of Course:
from 1:30 to 24:00

6 TUESDAY

Moon Void of Course:
from 0:00 to 5:07 ♋

7

WEDNESDAY

Moon Void of Course:
from 23:27 to 24:00

8

THURSDAY

Moon Void of Course:
from 0:00 to 7:24 ♌

9

FRIDAY

13:02 ☽ 16 ♌ 52

10

SATURDAY

Moon Void of Course:
from 11:19 to 12:48 ♍

Against the red ones
religions will unite
The rose (color) upon the middle
of the world scene...
To speak the truth they will have
closed mouths.
Then at the time of need the awaited
one will come late.

SCORPIO
Rules the genitals
Identity: The Healer
Keyword: Determined
Keynote: I desire

11 SUNDAY

☉	18 ♏	20
☿	0 ♐	0
♀	20 ♏	41
♂	11 ♓	19
♃	13 ♌	0
♄	20 ♉	36
♅	6 ♉	56
♆	12 ♉	26
♇	17 ♏	44

12 MONDAY

Moon Void of Course:
from 6:24 to 21:08 ♎

13 TUESDAY

14

WEDNESDAY

Moon Void of Course:
from 13:40 to 24:00

15

THURSDAY

Moon Void of Course:
from 0:00 to 7:39 ♏

16

FRIDAY

17

SATURDAY

9:05 ● 24 ♏ 45

Moon Void of Course:
from 17:58 to 19:39 ♐

might have done far more good than harm.

But as always, this will be discovered in time.

Among the many hundreds of prophets and Masters in our past, there have been common themes about the future of man's religious life and one of the most exciting is that which was given to us by Gautama the Buddha. His proposal was that every two-thousand five hundred years there would be the turn of what he called *The Wheel of Dharma*, a metaphorical wheel of time that turns and brings new changes to man.

The last such turn, according to the Buddhist beliefs was two thousand five hundred years ago, bringing the next turn to happen at the end of this century.

If we believe such Eastern philosophies then we are due for a major upheaval at the year 2,000 or thereabouts and this too coincides with the other predictions that the Catholic Church would die and a new awakening, together with a new religion would arise in the next millennium.

There is, of course, no scientific proof of any of this, but the writings of such Masters as Buddha and others coincide in their predictions and perhaps during this century of the New Age we may begin to understand unreasonable advice of this kind.

There have evidently recently been certain invitations for Bhagwan Shree Rajneesh to return to Europe. Now that all the fuss has died down a little surrounding his problems in America and one of the quatrains from "The Centuries" outlines the prophecy that the new religious leader will be at home in Europe.

Once again perhaps we will see, between this year's Date Book and next, another prophecy fulfilled.

In the meantime, the chart on page 175 of this book and within the original *Nostradamus and the Millennium* gives stars to indicate each of the "qualifications" for the expected religious leader that Nostradamus indicated. Bhagwan Shree Rajneesh seems to come out on top!

Second to the last of prophet's name
Will take Diana's day
(the moon's day)
as his day of silent rest...

SAGITTARIUS
November 22nd – December 20th
Mutable – Fire
Positive – Extrapersonal
Rules the 9th House
Ruled by Jupiter

☉	25 ♏	23
☿	10 ♐	29
♀	29 ♏	29
♂	9 ♓	1 ℞
♃	13 ♌	21
♄	21 ♉	9
♅	7 ♉	16
♆	12 ♉	37
♇	18 ♏	1

18 SUNDAY

Moon Void of Course:
from 22:46 to 24:00

19 MONDAY

Moon Void of Course:
from 0:00 to 24:00

20 TUESDAY

Moon Void of Course:
from 0:00 to 8:31 ♉

21
WEDNESDAY

22
THURSDAY

Moon Void of Course:
from 4:06 to 21:07 ≈

23
FRIDAY

24
SATURDAY

Moon Void of Course:
from 12:17 to 24:00

...many rare birds will cry
in the air.
"Now!" "Now!"
and sometime later will vanish.

SAGITTARIUS
South node in exaltation
Venus strong
Mercury in detriment
North node in fall

25 SUNDAY

13:11 ◑ 3 ♓ 0

Moon Void of Course:
from 0:00 to 7:32 ♓

☉ 2 ♐ 27
☿ 20 ♐ 37
♀ 8 ♐ 16
♂ 6 ♓ 25 ℞
♃ 13 ♌ 33
♄ 21 ♑ 46
♅ 7 ♑ 37
♆ 12 ♑ 49
♇ 18 ♏ 18

26 MONDAY

27 TUESDAY

Moon Void of Course:
from 2:45 to 14:06 ♈

28
WEDNESDAY

29
THURSDAY

Moon Void of Course:
from 11:18 to 16:37 ☿

30
FRIDAY

DECEMBER

*Before the moon has finished
her entire cycle (1889-2250),
the Sun (20th century) and then
Saturn (Aquarian Age) will come,
According to the Celestial signs
the reign of Saturn will come
a second time (Capricorn Age),
so that all is calculated,
the world draws near
to its final death dealing cycle.*

SAGITTARIUS
Stone: Topaz
Metal: Tin
Color: Purple

Being ruled by the expanding planet of Jupiter you are cheerful, optimistic, active and independent. You radiate enthusiasm, openness and are always ready for some more fun. Wonderful companions, you love to make others laugh. Idealistic and a seeker of truth you own a wonderful intuition.

Outspoken and frank you often insult or embarrass more sensitive people with straight forward remarks. To you it may be the most normal thing to say, not realizing that to others it is not.

Ruled by the Fire element, you love change, adventure and even danger. Most likely you will change profession and partner at least once if not more in your lifetime. You are restless and tend to dissipate your energies on too many projects.

Your constantly questioning mind leads you into many different fields and places, in some of you the Sagittarian essence of the seeker is expressed while in others it is turned inward. Either you are constantly going somewhere or on the look for new and interesting places to discover, or you can be found in the philosophers, mystics, seers and prophets. And it is often found that the Sagittarian women are the outward seekers and the men the inner seekers.

Rebels against injustice, corruption and authority, you don't care so much about morals and honesty, to you the important factors are truth and justice. You make excellent judges and social workers and your fancy in passing knowledge onto others makes you excell in teaching and lecturing. Your tendency to single pointedness may become exaggerated and lead you to fanaticism, a dogmatic attitude and the tendency to depend on religions ritual.

Because of the Sagittarian longing for truth, the soul travels along the road of the seeker. Lots of wonderful visions are coming to him, but he now needs the perseverance of the Capricorn to make his dreams come true. When the Sagittarius takes the responsibility already assumed by his following Sun sign, his philosophy will not be only spoken words.

THE LAST PREDICTIONS

Nostradamus predicts that the Aquarian age will dominate human consciousness around the end of the current lunar cycle at approximately 2250 A.D.

I N THE LAST CHAPTER of this Date Book we look quickly at perhaps Nostradamus' most dramatic and sweeping predictions – those that span thousands of years into our future. These quatrains are of particular significance for they give us a broader view of our world's future than any others.

The prophet has no problem in viewing life on a vast scale and his vision reaches out even to the end of the world – which he says will happen much sooner than we have envisaged in our own scientific projections.

The last years of this millennium will be perhaps the most significant in deciding what will occur thereafter, for if the possible "holocaust" does come about then the future will turn out to be very different than if there is no mass suicide.

The quatrains look at both alternatives, stating clearly enough that if man transcends the material level and manages not to murder himself, there are great rewards to be found thereafter.

Specifically he looked at the "Ages of Man" related to the astrological cycles. We are presently moving through the transition between the Age of Pisces and the Age of Aquarius which Nostradamus predicted would contain a thousand years of peace from 2026 to 3000. Following this major cycle comes the Age of Capricorn which the prophet saw as the last age of mankind, the Earth finally ending its life in the year 3797 precisely!

He goes on to say, however, that mankind will survive the final conflagration of the planet Earth and colonize space during the Age of Sagittarius between 6000 and 8000, to live throughout the universe as a powerful force for life everywhere.

"Before the moon has finished her entire cycle, the sun and then Saturn will come. According to the celestial signs the reign of Saturn will come a second time, so that all is calculated, the world draws near to its final death dealing cycle."

1

SATURDAY

Moon Void of Course:
from 4:20 to 16:23 ♓

2

SUNDAY

7:50 ○ 9 ♓ 52

Moon Void of Course:
from 20:48 to 24:00

☉	9	♐	32
☿	29	♐	59
♀	17	♐	4
♂	3	♓	49 ℞
♃	13	♌	35 ℞
♄	22	♑	25
♅	7	♑	59
♆	13	♑	3
♇	18	♏	34

3

MONDAY

Moon Void of Course:
from 0:00 to 15:27 ♋

4

TUESDAY

5

WEDNESDAY

Moon Void of Course:
from 4:00 to 16:00 ♌

6

THURSDAY

7

FRIDAY

Moon Void of Course:
from 8:39 to 19:39 ♍

8

SATURDAY

At the place Jason built his ship
(Greece)
There will be such a great
and sudden flood
That one will have no place
or land to fall upon,
The waves crest over Mount Olympus
(9,570 feet).

SAGITTARIUS
Animal: Stag
Bird: Eagle
Fish: Dolphin
Plant: Elm

☉	16 ♐	38
☿	7 ♑	24
♀	25 ♐	51
♂	1 ♓	28 ℞
♃	13 ♌	28 ℞
♄	23 ♉	7
♅	8 ♑	23
♆	13 ♑	17
♇	18 ♏	50

9 SUNDAY

2:04 ◑ 16 ♏ 44
Moon Void of Course:
from 21:14 to 24:00

10 MONDAY

Moon Void of Course:
from 0:00 to 3:00 ♎

11 TUESDAY

12 WEDNESDAY

Moon Void of Course:
from 0:28 to 13:28 ♏

13 THURSDAY

14 FRIDAY

15 SATURDAY

Moon Void of Course:
from 1:22 to 1:44 ♐

When the seventh millennium
has come (2000 A.D.)
There will then be a hecatomb
which will occur close
to the millennium end
Then those who entered the tomb
will leave.

SAGITTARIUS
Rules thighs
Identity: The Explorer
Keyword: Freedom
Keynote: I seek

16 SUNDAY

☉	23	♐	45
☿	9	♑	54 ℞
♀	4	♑	38
♂	29	♈	36 ℞
♃	13	♌	11 ℞
♄	23	♑	52
♅	8	♑	47
♆	13	♑	32
♇	19	♏	5

17 MONDAY

4:22 ● 24 ♐ 58

Moon Void of Course:
from 4:22 to 14:35 ♑

18 TUESDAY

19 WEDNESDAY

20 THURSDAY

Moon Void of Course:
from 0:37 to 2:59 ≈

21 FRIDAY

22 SATURDAY

Moon Void of Course:
from 10:47 to 13:48 ⅟

*Some will live in Aquarius
other in Cancer
for a longer time.*

CAPRICORN
December 21st – January 19th
Cardinal – Earth
Negative – Extrapersonal
Rules the 10th House
Ruled by Saturn

23 SUNDAY

☉ 0 ♑ 53
☿ 4 ♑ 2 ℞
♀ 13 ♑ 26
♂ 28 ♍ 22 ℞
♃ 12 ♌ 45 ℞
♄ 24 ♑ 38
♅ 9 ♑ 11
♆ 13 ♑ 47
♇ 19 ♏ 19

24 MONDAY

Moon Void of Course:
from 18:25 to 21:45 ♈

25 TUESDAY

3:16 ◑ 3 ♈ 4

26 WEDNESDAY

Moon Void of Course:
from 23:54 to 24:00

27 THURSDAY

Moon Void of Course:
from 0:00 to 2:09 ♉

28 FRIDAY

Moon Void of Course:
from 23:57 to 24:00

29 SATURDAY

Moon Void of Course:
from 0:00 to 3:26 ♓

30 SUNDAY

Moon Void of Course:
from 19:07 to 24:00

⊙ 8 ♑ 1
☿ 25 ♐ 34 ℞
♀ 22 ♑ 13
♂ 27 ♈ 48 ℞
♃ 12 ♌ 10 ℞
♄ 25 ♑ 26
♅ 9 ♑ 37
♆ 14 ♑ 3
♇ 19 ♏ 32

31 MONDAY

18:35 ○ 9 ♋ 50

Moon Void of Course:
from 0:00 to 3:02 ♋

IF NOSTRADAMUS HAD

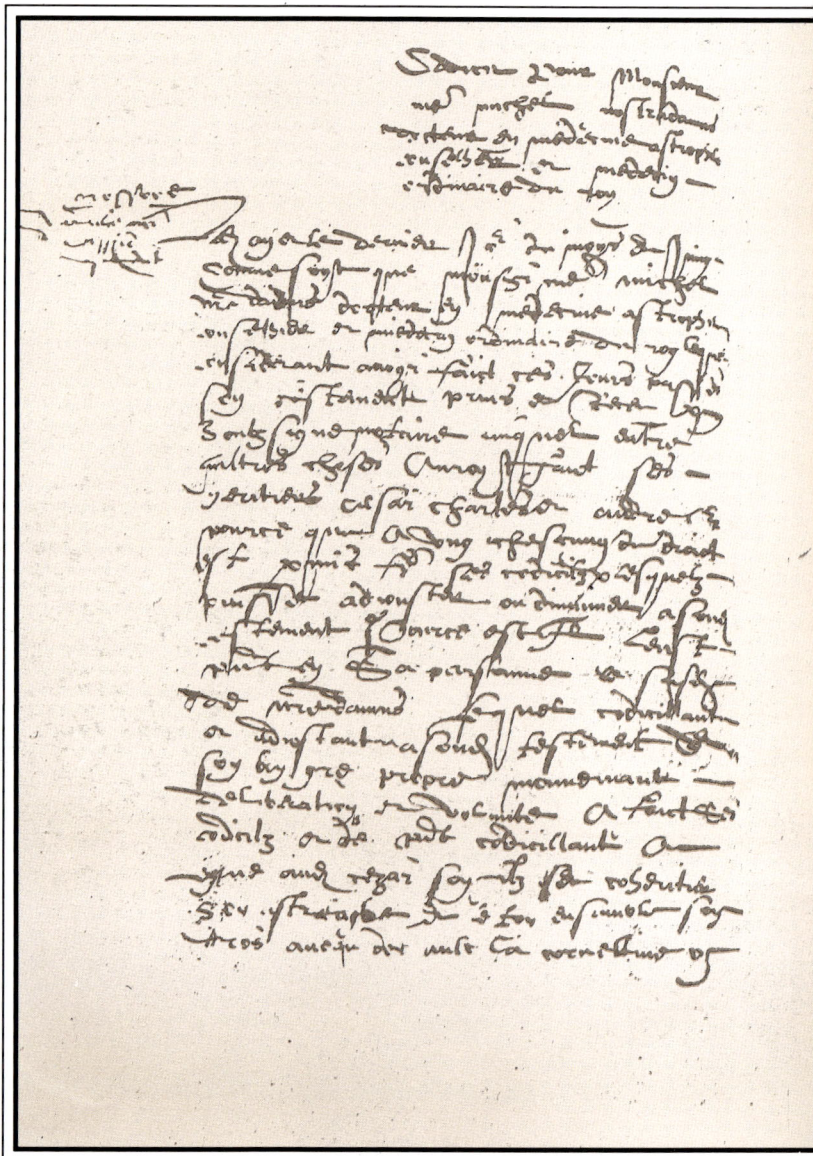

THE CENTURIES in its complete set of original volumes in effect forms a diary, written by one astonishing man over a few brief years of his own life. In scope, these years encompassed millennia of history in a form that can barely be conceived by those of us whose minds restrict us to our own generations and those we read about.

Among the many modern theories of "time" as a living dimension, it is proposed that we contain the past, present and future not in

WRITTEN A DIARY...

Nostradamus' handwriting.

a linear form, passing through one into the other and then forward step by step, but collateraly. Time exists within us all, from beginning to end as one. Could we but see it and conceive of it, our future lies alongside our past, now. Nostradamus did conceive this, throughout his prophetic years, each night, by the candle light of his upper rooms, and in the trances of his gifted understanding. This last chapter is therefore an effort to crystallize the main events contained in "The Centuries."

TIME	EVENT	DIARY ENTRY
8.00 p.m. one evening late 1544 **The Chateau of Lord de Florinville.** **At dinner with roasted pig.**	LORD FLORINVILLE BELIEVED he could test the prophet's powers by cheating. Nostradamus knew that of the two pigs which might be served for supper, only the black one would reach his table and the white would be eaten by a pet wolf. Florinville lost the test.	*"We will eat the black pig, but a wolf will eat the white."*
July 10th, 1559	THE DEATH OF KING HENRY II of France in a jousting accident on the rue St. Antoine outside Paris, at the hands of Count de Montgomery, whose lance pierced the kings visor.	*The young lion will overcome the older one* *On the field of combat in single battle.* *He will pierce his eyes through a cage of gold* *Two wounds made one, then he dies a cruel death.* C1 Q35
The night of July 1st 1566	NOSTRADAMUS' DEATH. Nostradamus called Father Vidal, the Superior of the Franciscan monastery in Salon, on July 1st, 1566 to hear the prophet's last confession and perform the last rites. Suffering from dropsy, an acute form of gout, Nostradamus spent the night alone and was found *"dead near the bed and the bench,"* in his room, by Chavigny, his assistant, the following morning.	*On his return from the Embassy, the King's gift put in place.* *He will do nothing more. He will be gone to God.* *Close relatives, friends, brothers by blood* *(Will find him) completely dead near the bed and the bench.* Presage 141

TIME	EVENT	DIARY ENTRY
1587	THE EXECUTION OF MARY STUART at Fotheringay after fleeing across "the river" between Europe and England.	*The great Queen will see herself conquered... she will pass over the river pursued by the sword.* *She will have outraged her faith.*
August 2nd, 1589	THE ASSASSINATION OF HENRY III of France at the hands of a Dominican friar, who answered a call to regicide and entered the King's bedchamber, an unsuspected man of God. Friar Clément went close to the King and drew a dagger, killing the unwanted sovereign and then dying on the swords of the guards.	*That which fire and sword could not accomplish* *Will be managed by a sweet speaking tongue in council:* *The King will be made to contemplate the dream seen while sleeping,* *He will see the enemy not in war or military blood.* C1 Q97
1658-1961	THE RISE AND FALL of the British Empire. Nostradamus saw how the British Empire would rise to power and then lose its great territories over a three hundred year period, all predicted in one short quatrain.	*A great empire will be for England* *The all powerful one through the sea for more than three hundred years:* *Great forces will pass by land and sea,* *The Portuguese will not be satisfied.* C10 Q100
1666	THE GREAT FIRE of London. The prophet saw the Fire of London as a divine retribution for the execution of Charles I. The *"ancient lady"* in the quatrain is the dome of St. Paul's Cathedral which collapsed during the fire from the heat, falling upon the heads of the faithful who sought shelter from the firestorm which devoured their homes.	*The blood of the just will be demanded of London* *Burnt by fire in the year '66.* *The ancient lady will fall from her high place,* *And many of the same sect will be killed.* C2 Q51

Time	Event	Diary Entry
1700	THE CITY FATHERS OF SALON decided to move the illustrious corpse of the prophet to a more prominent wall of the church where it was entombed. During the removal they took a quick look inside and found a practical joke which had taken one hundred and thirty-four years for the punchline: on his skeleton hung a medallion with the year 1700 inscribed.	
1791 **One night during the French Revolution.**	NATIONAL GUARDSMEN OF THE FRENCH Revolution broke into the Church where Nostradamus' tomb lay and during a drunken encounter tore open the stone slab and scattered the prophet's bones in all directions. One soldier drank wine from the skull, believing that this would imbue him with the powers of the prophet. The following day this man was shot dead by a sniper's bullet in an ambush.	*The man who opens the tomb when it is found* *And who does not close it immediately,* *Evil will come to him that no one will be able to prove.* C9 Q7
July 14th, 1789	THE FRENCH REVOLUTION – storming of the Bastille. For ten days following the liberation of the Bastille in Paris, lines of people touring the fortress filed past a table upon which lay a copy of one of the volumes of "The Centuries" open to the preface where all could read the prophet's words written two hundred and seventy-three years before, predicting the Revolution.	*Before the war comes, the great wall will fall,* *The King will be executed, his death coming too soon will be lamented.* *(The guards) will swim in blood,* *Near the River Seine the soil will be bloodied.* C2 Q57

TIME	EVENT	DIARY ENTRY
15th, August 1769	THE BIRTH OF NAPOLEON BONAPARTE. Nostradamus' first anti-christ.	*An emperor will be born near Italy. He will cost his empire dearly; they will say that from the sort of people who surround him that he is less a prince than a butcher.* C1 Q60
1889.	THE BIRTH OF HITLER. Nostradamus saw Hitler as the second anti-christ and possibly the greatest demagogue in our history. The prophet's belief was that each of the three anti-christs named would, in escalating degree, bring humanity closer to the final holocaust. Hitler, named as "Hister," was responsible for the death of fifty million people during a six year war costing the world billions of dollars. He set standards of horror that even modern statesmen would find hard to equal.	*From the deepest part of Western Europe,* *A young child will be born to poor people:* *Who by his speech will seduce a great multitude,* *His reputation will increase in the Kingdom of the East.* C3 Q35
The 20th Century	NOSTRADAMUS SAW THE 20TH CENTURY as an evil and mechanized time in which every one would be numbered, recorded, catagorized and organized.	*Before long everything will be organized* *We await a very evil century:* *The lot of the masked and solitary ones (clergy) greatly changed,* *Few will be found who wish to stay in their places.* C2 Q10

TIME	EVENT	DIARY ENTRY
1930s	THE BUILDING OF THE MAGINOT LINE. In its certainty of protection and security, the Maginot Line was one of the great farces of military history, built in the 1930s to protect the borders of France against all comers, at a cost of two million dollars (1930 values), it stretched one hundred and ninety-five miles in a network of forts. The forts were sunk seven floors into the ground with interconnecting underground railways. Fifteen rivers broke the line and Hitler's army entered France through Belgium and not Switzerland as believed.	*Near the great river, a vast trench, earth excavated,* *It will be divided by water into fifteen parts:* *the city taken, fire blood, cries and battle given* *The greater part of the people concerned with the collision.* C4 Q80
1958-1970	FRENCH PRESIDENT CHARLES DE GAULLE.	*...for three times one surnamed de Gaulle will lead France...* C9 Q33
Noon, November 22nd, 1963	ASSASSINATION OF JOHN F. KENNEDY in Dallas Texas. Nostradamus not only saw the tragic death of a man who could have become America's greatest leader, but he saw, seemingly in detail, events and people that no one today is yet certain of — the true killers.	*The ancient work will be accomplished,* *And from the roof evil ruin will fall on the great man.* *Being dead they accuse an innocent of the deed:* *the guilty one is hidden in the misty woods.* C6 Q37
October, 1973	THE YOM KIPPUR WAR. On the 6th of October, 1973 at just before 2.00 p.m., both Egypt and Syria attacked Israel without warning and began what is for Nostradamus, the beginning of World War III, a war that will continue for twenty-seven years until the end of the millennium.	*A race that has always overcome hazards,* *And which has not feared war,* *In the country which lies close to Christianity's end,* *Will be shocked by an act committed by Egypt* *Whose people will rejoice at it.* Sixtain 31

Time	Event	Diary Entry
1979-2000	**A NEW RELIGIOUS CONSCIOUSNESS.** Nostradamus' predictions on the brighter side of our future center around a new religious consciousness which he dates as beginning sometime in the late 70s and growing to a peak of acceptance in the mid-90s. There are many quatrains surrounding what appears to be one man who brings eloquent speech, red colors and birds that fly in the sky. All this may seem somewhat cryptic to us now but there is already at least one religious leader alive who could fit the description.	*A man will be charged with destroying the temples and religions altered by fantasy.* *He will harm the rocks rather than the living.* *Ears filled with ornate speeches.* *He will travel far and wide in his drive to infuriate, delivering a great people from subjection.* *He will fly through the sky, the rains and the snows* *And strike everyone with his rod.* C2 Q28 C1 Q96 C2 Q29
The 1980s	**THE THIRD ANTI-CHRIST** was named directly by Nostradamus, as were the first and the second. If we are to accept his "system" of warning us of our future trends, then it is possible that this third "demagogue" lives today and is named "Mabus".	*Mabus* will soon die, then will come A horrible slaughter of people and animals,* *At once vengeance is revealed coming from a hundred hands* *Thirst, and famine when the comet will pass.*
1986	**CHERNOBYL - THE LIVES** for one hundred thousand Ukrainians changed when the melt down created a radioactive cloud that would poison and destroy their lives and their futures. Nostradamus saw this as the beginning of the greatest change that Communism had ever seen since the beginning. The reference to "More" in the quatrain opposite uses Sir Thomas More, the author of Utopia, for socialism (Utopia was the first Socialist manifesto), tracing the Soviet changes from Czarist, through Communism to a happier order towards the end of this century.	*...The communial law will be made in opposition.* *The old order will hold strong, then are removed from the scene:* *Then Communism put far behind.* C4 Q32 *The law of More will be seen to decline,* *Followed by one more pleasing.* C3 Q95

*NB – Some editions of "The Centuries" show the name "Mabus" as "Malus" meaning evil or wicked. The name happens to appear at the beginning of a quatrain so that we cannot be sure whether Nostradamus intended this to be a specific name or a word, not capitalized, which means a series of evil people or deeds. The third anti-christ could therefore be simply terrorism.

Time	Event	Diary Entry
1990	SOVIET-US ALLIANCE. Though there is no clear dating of such an alliance, Nostradamus does make clear predictions of its happening. Using a method which may be somewhat random, the number of the quatrain most directly connected to such an alliance is 89.	*One day the great powers will become friends* *Their great power will be seen to increase.* *The new land (America) will be at the height of its power.* *To the man of blood (the anti-christ) the number is reported.* C2 Q89
September 1993	THE GREAT PESTILENCE – AIDS. The prophet spoke in some detail about another vast plague which would strike man and he aludes to it being a plague of the blood and of semen. The references are difficult to dispute in many cases and seem most closely to apply to the relatively new disease – Acquired Immune Deficiency Syndrome. According to Nostradamus' estimates this plague, in any event, will infect half the world by the mid-1990s.	*A horrible war which is being prepared in the West,* *The following year the pestilence will come,* *So very horrible that young nor old, nor animal (may survive).* *Blood, fire, Mercury, Mars, Jupiter in France. (September 1993)* C9 Q55
Mid-1990s	SUPERQUAKES HIT EARTH. Nostradamus sees and warns us of several series of superquakes which seem to strike Earth in a predictable pattern. One part of the series begins in the mid-1990s and spreads from the west coast of India rising to a crescendo through a broken Western United States. East Africa will be split into three pieces and New York and Florida will be flooded.	

SEQUENCE OF CATASTROPHES

1. *EARTHQUAKES AND TIDAL WAVES DEVASTATE INDIA*
2. *HEAVY EARTHQUAKES DESTROY PARTS OF JAPAN*
3. *MAJOR EARTHQUAKE IN ITALY, MOUNT VESUVIUS ERUPTS*
4. *MOUNT PELEE ON MARTINIQUE ERUPTS*
5. *EARTHQUAKES IN WESTERN NORTH-AMERICA*

TIME	EVENT	DIARY ENTRY
1995-1999	THE BREAKDOWN OF SOVIET-US ALLIANCES. The alliance between the two great superpowers does not last for long and probably breaks up during the latter part of the Third World War.	*The two will not remain allied for long,* *Within the thirteen years (1986-1999) they surrender to Barbare (Libya) and Iranian leaders* *There will be such loss on both sides,* *That one will bless Petrus Romanus (the end of millennium Pope).*
1996	THE ARAB ATTACK on the soft underbelly of Europe through Italy, by submarine.	*When weapons and plans are enclosed in a fish (submarine) in 1996,* *Out of it will come a man who will then make war,* *His fleet will have traveled far across the sea* *To appear at the Italian shore.* C2 Q5
1997	NEW YORK CITY under nuclear attack.	*The sky will burn at forty-five degrees (latitude of New York City).* *Fire approaches the New City.* *In an instant a huge scattered flame leaps up...* C6 Q97
July 1999	THE LAST CONFLAGRATION. Nostradamus dates the holocaust at "1999 and seven months." This will be the culmination of the twenty seven years of war and the final destruction of the civilized world.	*In the year 1999 and seven months* *The great King of Terror will come from the sky* *He will resurrect Ghengis Khan* *Before and after war rules happily.* C10 Q72

TIME	EVENT	DIARY ENTRY
Easter 2000	THE FLOODING OF ENGLAND. England, or at least the southern part of it, will sink beneath the sea at Easter of the year 2000. Other prophets such as Edgar Cayce have also mirrored this quatrain.	*A trembling of the earth at Mortara, The tin islands of St. George half sunk: Drowsy with peace, war will awaken, The abyss of the temple ripped open at Easter.* C9 Q31
2026-3000	A THOUSAND YEARS OF PEACE. The prophet predicts one thousand years of peace in which a galactic community becomes a reality and man enters a period where science and religion merge into a higher consciousness. In this period, towards its end he warns of too much knowledge turning us toward selfishness and the manipulation of others.	*When the seventh millennium has come (2000 A.D.) There will then be a hecatomb which will occur close to the millennium end. Then those who entered the tomb will leave.* C10 Q74
4000-6000 The Age of Capricorn.	THE FINAL PHASE ON EARTH. Nostradamus, in his last predictions sees man either destroyed finally or transcending the material plane. The 27th century after Christ will see this theme influencing the dying Aquarian Age. The year 3755 brings vast meteor showers and in his preface to his son Caesar, he tells him that the Earth will finally end in the year 3797.	*Before the moon has finished her entire cycle (1889-2250), the sun (20th century)and then Saturn (Aquarian Age) will come. According to the celestial signs the reign of Saturn will come a second time (Capricorn Age), so that all is calculated, the world draws near to its final death dealing cycle.* Preface to Caesar.
6000-8000 — The Age of Sagittarius.	THE AGE OF TRUTH. Nostradamus tells us that in the final analysis the human race survives planet Earth's conflagration. He indicates that we will colonize space and live in ever increasing numbers throughout the universe.	*Some will live in Aquarius others in Cancer for a longer time.*

NOTES

NOTES

ACKNOWLEDGEMENTS

ALINARI, Florence, Italy: 79 (right)

GRAZIA NERI, Milan, Italy: 93, 102, 102/103, 109 (left), 110/111, 118/119, 119, 128, 142/143, 174 (middle & right), 175 (right), 80

THE IMAGE BANK, Milan, Italy: 94/95, 159 (top)

K & B NEWS, Florence, Italy: 134/135, 157, 166/167

LUIGI VOLPE, Milan, Italy: 109 (right)

BBC HULTON LIBRARY, London, England: 96, 174 (left)

BRUCE COLEMAN, London, England: 182/183

FRANKL J.: 86

IMPERIAL WAR MUSEUM, London, England: 77 (top & center), 125

THE NATIONAL PORTRAIT GALLERY, London, England: 42, 43 (except Hitler)

YOUNG ARTISTS, London, England: 190/191, 201

ROGER VIOLLET, Paris, France: 30/31, 46/47, 48, 54, 55, 61, 62/63, 70/71, 75, 77 (bottom), 79 (left), 141, 160

SUSAN B. MORGAN: illustrations of the Sun signs.

Janvier

```
 1   2   3   4   5   6   7
 8   9  10  11  12  13  14
15  16  17  18  19  20  21
22  23  24  25  26  27  28
29  30  31
```

Fevrier

```
 1   2   3   4   5   6   7
 8   9  10  11  12  13  14
15  16  17  18  19  20  21
22  23  24  25  26  27  28
```

May

```
 1   2   3   4   5   6   7
 8   9  10  11  12  13
15  16  17  18  19
22  23  24  25  26
29  30  31
```

Juin

```
 1   2   3   4   5   6   7
 8   9  10  11  12  13  14
         18  19  20  21
     23  24  25  26  27  28
29  23
```

September

```
 1   2   3   4   5   6   7
 8   9  10  11  12  13  14
15  16  17  18  19  20  21
22  23  24  25  26  27  28
29  30
```

October

```
 1   2   3   4   5   6   7
 8   9  10  11  12  13  14
15  16  17  18  19  20  21
22  23  24  25  26  27  28
29  30  31
```